Even More TALKS FOR CHILDREN

Compiled and edited by

Ian MacLeod

with Contributions from

Ian MacLeod

David Harbison

Richard Coley

Gordon McColl

D Ross Mitchell

Iain Roy

SAINT ANDREW PRESS

Edinburgh

First published in 1997 by
SAINT ANDREW PRESS
121 George Street, Edinburgh EH2 4YN

Copyright © Ian MacLeod (compiler and editor) 1997

ISBN 0 7152 0724 5

British Library Cataloguing in Publication Data
A catalogue record for this book
is available from the British Library.

ISBN 0715207245

Cover design by Mark Blackadder.
Typesetting by Lesley A Taylor.
Printed and **bound** by Athenaeum Press Ltd, Gateshead, Tyne & Wear.

Contents

Part 2
THE FAMILY SERVICE
by Iain Roy

Foreword

MY late friend, the **Revd J I MacDonald** – a specialist in Religious Education, a contributor to the previous volume in this series *More Talks for Children* (Saint Andrew Press), and latterly a member of Brodick Church – used to speak in good-natured fashion of the ephemeral nature of many Children's Addresses which he had heard over a lifetime. To him, it was sad when the great truths of the Gospel were obscured by the gimmicky and the trivial.

In preparing the present volume, that thought has been much in my mind. For that reason, I am grateful to the contributors within, whose dedication to communicating the Gospel, whether to children or adults, would not allow them to devalue it in that way.

Richard Coley is minister at Tollcross Victoria Church in Glasgow, **David Harbison** is minister of Beith High and Trinity, and **Iain Roy** is minister at Livingstone Church in Stevenston. Each of them also contributed to the last volume. I am equally grateful to **D Ross Mitchell**, minister of St Andrew's, West Kilbride, and to **Gordon McColl**, for their welcome contributions to this work.

All the material enclosed has been included in the hope that, like the previous volumes (*Talks for Children* and *More Talks for Children*), the present one may be of use to others as they strive to communicate the faith to the young.

A special thanks must go to **Iain Roy** who has kindly contributed a separate section on 'The Family Service', supplying some splendid examples; and, for my part, I am grateful to Saint Andrew Press for the opportunity to contribute to, and to compile and edit this book.

Ian MacLeod 1997

Part 1

Even More
TALKS
FOR CHILDREN

The Windscreen Sticker

◆ TEXT – Amos 5: 23-24
> 'Take away from me the noise of your songs;
>> to the melody of your harps I will not listen.
> But let justice roll down like waters,
>> and righteousness like an ever flowing stream.'

◆ VISUAL AID (if required) –
A windscreen sticker illustrative of any of the types mentioned below

DO you ever read the stickers that people attach to their cars? What interesting and amusing messages they can carry!

Some of them tell of people's loyalties – stickers like that usually have a heart in the middle informing us that the car owner loves some particular thing or place. I have seen lots, for example, which say, 'I love Arran'. Or sometimes the sticker warns the driver behind, stating that a car has a child as a passenger. Indeed, some of these warnings can be rather cheeky, telling you that if you can actually *read* the sticker, then you are following too closely and should slow down and give the car in front space. Occasionally a sticker shows that a driver has a sense of humour, like the one on a small car which says: 'When I grow up, I'm going to be a Rolls Royce'!

I once saw a huge petrol tanker that had a sticker on the back of it which I had never seen before. On a yellow background, in very large letters, it carried the message: 'I'm not deaf. I'm just ignoring you.'

The more I thought about it, the more I could understand the driver of that tanker. Here was a heavy vehicle which normally travelled long

2

distances on the motorway. Most often its driver would be in the inside lane, but now and again he would meet a whole chain of even heavier lorries lumbering along ahead of him. Then he would move into the middle lane and begin to overtake. But having taken up his new position, sometimes a fast car would come up behind with an impatient driver at the wheel. The impatient driver would follow for a few seconds, and then he would begin to sound his horn, hoping that the tanker driver would immediately move back into the inside lane just to let him past. I suspect this had happened so often that the tanker driver got fed up and bought a sticker which said: 'I'm not deaf. I'm just ignoring you.'

That sticker was a way of telling impatient drivers that a lorry has a right to be on the road and to receive the same consideration as any other road user. It was a way of reminding discourteous and selfish motorists that this driver would not be hurried or worried by them. He could hear them perfectly well, but he would not heed their rudeness.

One of the Old Testament prophets said that there are times when even God ignores people. His name was Amos, and he lived at a time when many seemed only interested in themselves and thought nothing of harassing the helpless and the poor. So long as they were getting ahead, it didn't matter about anyone who could not keep up with them. And yet these same selfish people still expected God to listen to them.

That is when the prophet spoke for God, and when he did there was anger in his voice: *'Take away from me the noise of your songs; to the melody of your harps I will not listen.'* And then he went on: *'But let justice roll down like waters, and righteousness like an ever flowing stream.'*

Amos reminded the selfish people of his day, as he would also remind us, that when we are selfish and unkind to other people, then we have no right to expect God to accept our worship. God, who is not deaf, will just ignore us. When we are considerate of others and when we treat them kindly, then we have a right to expect God to listen to us.

◆ PRAYER –
Lord God, help us so to live, mindful of the needs of others, that Your ear may ever be open to hear our prayers, our worship and our praise. In Jesus' name. Amen.

The Floating Church

◆ TEXT – Psalm 122: 1 (Revised English Bible)
'I rejoiced when they said to me,
"Let us go to the house of the Lord!"'

AROUND the coast of Scotland many of our churches are situated by the sea. But have you ever heard of a church which actually *floated* in the sea? A church just like that was built 150 years ago.

In the middle of the last century, many people, for a number of reasons, left the Church of Scotland to attend what became known as the Free Church of Scotland. In the area of Strontian in Argyll, those who had left the old church to join the new were anxious to have a church building of their own. The landowner, however, was a staunch member of the Church of Scotland and would allow no Free Church to be built on his land.

For some time the new congregation simply met for worship in the open air. This was all right so long as the weather was warm and sunny, but when it was cold and wet and windy it was most uncomfortable. So, eventually, the people began to consider what else they might do. Then the suggestion was made of a floating church which might be anchored in a sheltered bay near a beach and to which worshippers could travel by small boats. Some people laughed at the idea, but others were sure that it could be done.

Plans were prepared, and it was soon clear that the scheme was possible. Prices were obtained, the money was raised, and the work was given to one of the building yards on the River Clyde, under the supervision of Robert Brown of Fairlie.

Eventually it was completed and the floating church was towed all the way down the River Clyde by two tug boats. It passed Arran, sailed round the Mull of Kintyre, up the sound of Jura, along the Sound of Mull, and finally into Loch Sunart where it was moored about 150 yards off shore.

Made of iron, the floating church had a vestry and covered pulpit in the bow, and the minister, who arrived by boat, entered it at that end. The congregation also arrived by boat and 'came aboard' at the stern, the whole area being filled with benches to seat 750 people, with a single passage-way up the middle to allow them to move in and out.

Sometimes the church was busier than others, and the congregation soon found an exciting way of counting how many people were present. They discovered that the church's hull sank one inch lower in the water for every hundred people present. If it went down two inches, there were two hundred at worship. If it went down six inches, there were six hundred present. Sometimes there were over 700 attending, and one minister who led worship had the honour of being told by the elders that no one had ever caused their church to sink so low before!

If our church floated, how far do you think it would sink in the water on Sunday morning? And would we always be there to help it?

The Old Testament Psalmist once said of the Jewish temple: '*I rejoiced when they said to me, "Let us go to the house of the Lord!"*' If we are like him – whether our church is a floating church or an ordinary one that stands on solid ground – we will always be happy to play our part in filling it, so that God may be given the praise and the worship that He is due.

◆ PRAYER –
Lord God, we thank You for Your Church. Grant us now and always to find Your worship not a duty but a joy. In Jesus' name. Amen.

The
Dreamcatcher

◆ TEXT – Joel 2: 28
*'... your old men shall dream dreams,
and your young men shall see visions.'*

IF you ever visit an Indian reservation in Canada or America, you will discover that the Indian people are very skillful with their hands. Because of that, reservations often have a shop where visitors can buy the goods which the Indian craftsmen and women have made. There you will find jewellery, especially turquoise rings, pendants and bracelets. You will find very beautiful paintings. You will find Indian head-dresses with brightly coloured feathers. You will find tomahawks and drums and dolls dressed in Indian costume, and, always, you will find an item which is known as a 'dreamcatcher'.

When an Indian boy or girl is born, a dreamcatcher is made by family or friends and it is hung above the child's bed. It will be his or hers for life, and when life is over it is buried with them.

The dreamcatcher comes in various sizes, but its form is always the same. It hangs by a leather or suede thong. Suspended from the thong is a leather circle, the centre of which is filled with little gut strings (the material of violin strings) so that the inside of the circle looks rather like a spider's web. One or two of these strings have tiny beads threaded onto them, while others have brightly coloured feathers passing through them.

The Indians believe that the dreamcatcher will do for the child exactly what its name suggests. It will catch his dreams. The dreams which are coming to the child will pass through the dreamcatcher before they

6

enter his or her mind. Then every bad dream will be caught in the web, just like the beads, so that the child will never experience it; while the good dreams, just like the feathers, will be allowed to pass through. In that way the child will only experience happy dreams.

It's a lovely custom, boys and girls, because none of us wants a bad dream, what we call a nightmare. That is the kind of experience we do not seek, and that is why one of the hymnwriters says in an evening hymn –

> *Let no ill dreams disturb my rest*
> *No powers of darkness me molest.*

The Bible has a lot to say about dreams, and it too is concerned that we might have good dreams. That is why the Old Testament writer once said, '*... your old men shall dream dreams, and your young men shall see visions*'. He was thinking especially of how God's Spirit will bring to men and women dreams of a better world.

Indeed many men and women have done a great deal to make the world a better and happier place, because God first put the idea of what they had to do into their mind. So let us ask God to give us that kind of dream, and with it the ability to make the dream come true.

◆ PRAYER –
Lord God; as we live, teach us what we should be and do, and give us the ability to do it and be it. In Jesus' name. Amen

The
'Betsy'

◆ TEXT – 1 Corinthians 9: 16 (Revised English Bible)
  'It would be agony for me not to preach.'

IN Scotland, ministers live in houses known as 'manses'. Some are very old. Some are very new. Some have large gardens. Some have small ones. Some are cold and draughty. Some are warm and cosy. But the strangest manse that any minister ever had must have been the one that had sails.

It happened in 1843 when many people on the island of Eigg, together with their minister, left the Church of Scotland to attend the Free Church. Since he now had to leave the Church of Scotland manse, the minister, a Mr Swanson, had nowhere to stay, although the people would gladly have built him a new home. But that was impossible, because the owner of the island belonged to the Church of Scotland and he refused to allow a Free Church manse to be built on his land. In fact, the nearest house to his old parish that Mr Swanson could find was miles across the sea on the island of Skye.

Determined not to be beaten, and eager to continue to care for his people, to visit them and preach to them on Eigg, the brave Mr Swanson moved his family to the house on Skye, while he himself bought a boat called the 'Betsy'. There, he lived and worked, and he spent so much time aboard travelling to and from and around Eigg that the boat became known as the 'floating manse'.

It sounds an exciting way to live. What inspiring sermons he would glean from the sea and the creatures living in it and from it!

On the other hand, it must have been difficult to sail a boat and write sermons at the same time, to say nothing of trying to read while the 'manse' bobbed up and down in the waves.

In fact, since the 'Betsy' was a small boat, it was an uncomfortable manse. Its cabin, which served as living quarters, kitchen, study and bedroom all in one, was only two metres broad and four long. Indeed, when it was cold, stormy or wet outside, as it often is in that part of Scotland, the hatch had to be pulled shut; and then, because the area inside was so small, it became unbearably hot.

When the Free Church Assembly met in Glasgow, in the autumn of 1843, the minister of Eigg announced that he would bring his manse with him. And so he did, because he sailed there in the 'Betsy'! In fact, the idea of a minister sailing his manse up the river to the city so caught the imagination of the people that many decided to visit the 'Betsy' as soon as she berthed.

That is when they discovered that the minister of Eigg was a brave man, for the 'Betsy' was a poor vessel, none too seaworthy, and unfit for use in an area exposed to the storms of the mighty Atlantic. Yet he accepted the risk for the sake of the work that he did.

Have you ever heard some news, and then, because it was such good news, discovered that nothing could stop you from sharing it. That was how Mr Swanson felt when he sailed in the 'Betsy'. Like Saint Paul, who once said *'It would be agony for me not to preach'*, nothing could stop him from spreading the good news of God's love among his people – not even the lack of a manse! The news that God loves us is as important as that, and it is just as important to share it with other people.

◆ PRAYER –
Lord God, we give You thanks for all who have heard Your call to preach the gospel – for ministers, missionaries and Sunday School teachers. Help us also to be ready to share the good news of Your love with others. In Jesus' name. Amen.

Blast-off
delayed

◆ TEXT – Song of Solomon 2: 15
'Catch us the foxes,
the little foxes
that spoil the vineyards.'

WHAT is the most powerful form of transport you can think of? Is it a mighty railway locomotive pulling dozens of wagons along a line? Is it an ocean liner ploughing its course through trackless seas? Is it a hover-craft carrying people and cars across the English Channel? Or is it a jumbo jet flying hundreds of passengers across the world?

The most powerful form of transport is the kind that is used for space travel. In fact, the power of the booster rocket used for all the American Apollo moon journeys was equal to that of fifty jumbo jets just on its own! That is why I was interested in something that happened recently to the space shuttle at Cape Canaveral in Florida.

The shuttle is a very powerful means of transport. Lifted by the thrust from its massive boosters, people and all kinds of equipment are launched miles into space, together with that huge glider which we know as the 'shuttle' for their safe return.

Some time ago, the shuttle 'Discovery' was on the launching pad, ready to blast off on a mission which was going to put a satellite into orbit. The brave astronauts were ready. The groundstaff were ready. The equipment to be transported was ready. But suddenly it was announced that the mission was being called off, because urgent repair work was required to the craft.

The space shuttle has a fuel tank on the outside, and the tank is protected by a layer of foam. On this occasion, just before the launch was due to take place, the foam jacket was found to have been punctured with lots of little holes – 205 of them in total. An examination was made to find out how they could have got there, and it was quickly discovered that the culprits were a pair of woodpeckers trying to build a nest by simply doing what they know how to do best of all – which is to peck holes with their chisel-shaped bills!

It may be hard to believe, but the evidence could not be doubted. The gigantic and powerful space shuttle had not only been brought to a standstill, but was delayed from its journey for *five* weeks, just because two tiny creatures had pecked holes in the protective layer over the fuel tank!

One of the Old Testament writers once spoke about catching *'the little foxes that spoil the vineyards'*. That was something he had seen himself. He knew the havoc that even a little fox could cause in a vineyard, gnawing at the vines with its teeth and spoiling the harvest of grapes. Just like those who prepare the space shuttle for blast-off at Cape Canaveral and who discovered the work of the woodpeckers, so he had discovered that little things are important because they have the power to destroy.

That is something we all learn. Just a little boasting or cheating or unkindness or lying has the power to spoil things for ourselves and for everybody else. And little things that do damage like that have to be prevented at all costs.

That is why the hymnwriter speaks about –

*'Leaving every day behind, something which might hinder
Running swifter every day, growing purer, kinder.'*

By the help of God, let's do our best to keep out of our lives the little things that cause all kinds of trouble, and let's ask for the things that make life better for ourselves and for others.

◆ PRAYER –
Lord God, as we live and grow, guide us by Your Holy Spirit that our lives may bring joy to others and to You. In Jesus' name. Amen.

Brad

◆ TEXT – Psalm 101: 6
'I will look with favour on the faithful in the land …'

DO you like trains? Years ago, when our trains were pulled by steam-powered locomotives, many a boy would spend a Saturday happily perched on a railway embankment, or sitting on a station platform, jotting down in a notebook the numbers on the side of all the locomotives which passed by.

Someone who loves trains today is called Brad. He lives in the state of Mississippi in the United States of America, and his home is close to a railroad where one of the great American trains runs all the way from New Orleans in the south to Chicago in the north. That train is known as the 'City of New Orleans'. Its journey – which takes a day and a half to complete – is almost a thousand miles long.

On route the scenery is constantly changing. Fields of cotton, with old colonial mansions nearby, remind you of bygone days, now happily gone, when slaves worked on the plantations. Endless acres of corn and wheat, and lonely farmsteads standing among them, make you think of those who work hard to provide food for the world. At one moment you are passing alligator-infested swamps or marshes filled with pelicans, and the next you are travelling through great cities like St Louis and Memphis and Kansas, or skirting great rivers like the Missouri and the Mississippi.

Again and again on that journey the train comes to level crossings where the line crosses a road. As it approaches each crossing, the engine whistles eerily, warning oncoming traffic of its presence. One of the

12

crossings is called 'Thayers' crossing. That is where Brad can be found, standing day after day, just waiting for the train to come. In fact, the passengers aboard the northbound 'City of New Orleans' are instructed to look out to the right, where they will find Brad waiting to wave to the train as it passes.

Brad has been doing this for so long that he has become part of the scenery himself. He is a great favourite with all who work on the route. Indeed, after they had noticed him standing faithfully at 'Thayers' crossing, morning and evening, month after month, whether the weather was wet or dry, the conductors and engine drivers one day decided to stop and invite him on board for a ride. Then they rewarded his faithful appearance and cheery wave by giving him presents. They gave him railway hats and railway uniform buttons and other mementos of the Amtrak railway system, and he is now regarded as the unofficial 'mascot' of the train called the 'City of New Orleans'.

It is always a great thing to be faithful, to be loyal and dependable in doing what is good and kind and encouraging to other people, and, as Brad was to discover to his joy, that kind of faithfulness seldom goes unnoticed.

Another man who knew this was the Psalmist of the Old Testament. He wanted to be sure that his people would never forget or fall away from God. He wanted them to be faithful and dependable in worshipping and serving Him. So, speaking for God, he wrote these words: *'I will look with favour on the faithful in the land.'*

God looks for all of us to be the kind of people who are reliable, and that kind of faithfulness never escapes his notice.

◆ PRAYER –
Lord God, Your goodness and faithfulness never end. Help us also to be the kind of people who can be counted on, so that our lives may reflect something of Your nature. In Jesus' name. Amen.

The
Silver Spoon

◆ TEXT – Ephesians 2: 4 (Authorised Version)
'God who is rich in mercy, for his great love wherewith he loved us.'

◆ VISUAL AID –
An Apostle teaspoon

HAVE you ever heard somebody say of another person, 'He was born with a silver spoon in his mouth'? That is a phrase we sometimes use to describe people who, right from their birth, have had every chance to do well without too many difficulties appearing in their way. But where does such a strange phrase come from?

Let's begin with this teaspoon which I have in my hand. [*Hold up spoon.*] This kind of spoon has a special name, although there are many just like it. In fact, you may even have one, or a whole set similar to this in your own home. Does anybody know the special name that is given to a spoon like this? .... That's it – it's called an 'Apostle teaspoon'.

These spoons are called this because of that little figure at the top of the stem. If you look at him closely, you can see that he has a head, and you can also see that he is wearing a long robe which hangs in very beautiful folds all the way down to his feet. He is meant to represent one of the apostles of Jesus, and an apostle was a friend of Jesus who was sent out to preach about him. That is why spoons like these, with a little figure like this on the stem, are known as 'Apostle teaspoons'.

At one time it was quite common to give an 'Apostle teaspoon' made of silver as a present for a baby after its baptism. Sometimes four were given, and they represented the four evangelists or gospel writers –

14

Matthew, Mark, Luke and John. Sometimes a set of twelve was given, and they represented the twelve disciples whose names are given in the Bible.

Anyway, because silver was expensive, 'Apostle teaspoons' made of silver tended to be given by fairly wealthy people, and the phrase which speaks about being 'born with a silver spoon in one's mouth', almost certainly refers to the child who was fortunate enough to be given such a gift at the time of his or her baptism.

I don't know, boys and girls, whether you were given an 'Apostle teaspoon' when you were baptised, or if anyone has ever said of you that you were 'born with a silver spoon in your mouth'. But each of us here who has been baptised has been given something more wonderful than that.

For we have received the promise that the love of God surrounds us all our lives, from our beginning until our end. We have received the sign of his forgiveness when we seek it honestly after we have done wrong, and the constant support of his people in the family of the Church.

One of the great apostles of Jesus once wrote about this, when he spoke of that *'great love wherewith God loved us'*. That is far better than a silver spoon or promises of an easy life.

◆ PRAYER –
Father in heaven, teach us that our true wealth lies not in the things that we possess, but in Your love for us. In Jesus' name. Amen.

King
Very-Well-Then

◆ TEXT – 1 Kings 18: 21
'How long will you go limping with two different opinions? If the Lord is God, follow him; but if Baal, then follow him.'

MOST boys and girls enjoy making choices. I wonder if you do? The answer probably depends on what is being offered. Some people, however, find it difficult to choose. They can never quite make up their minds. The result is that they never seem to get anywhere unless someone else makes their decisions for them.

Five hundred years ago there lived a prince like that. He was the eldest son of the King of Poland and his name was Vladislas. In 1471 he became Vladislas II, King of Bohemia, and then, 17 years later, King of Hungary too.

Vladislas is remembered in history as a weak man who found it difficult to make decisions. In fact he found it so hard to make up his mind on anything, that he was content to agree to whatever suggestions were made to him. Because he found it so difficult to choose, other people soon had him in their power, and in the end he was dominated by the nobles, the leading families in Hungary, who boasted that they had a king 'whose beard they could hold in their fists'.

To 'hold somebody's beard in your fist' means that, if he is to avoid pain, you can pull him around any way you want and anywhere you choose. So the Hungarian nobles were saying that their king was like that – just like a puppet on a string with no will of his own. They could control him and make him agree to whatever they wanted.

His favourite word was 'all right', and he would say it whether what

16

was being suggested was wise or not, good or not, or kind or not. Some-how he lacked the courage to make his own choice, to decide for himself and to stand by his decision.

It was for that reason that his subjects had little respect for him and gave him a cruel nickname. He became known as 'King Very-Well-Then', the man who could not make up his mind, who said, 'all right' or 'very-well-then' to everything, and who was quite content to be led by the suggestions of others.

There was a time when the people of Israel were a bit like King Very-Well-Then, for, living in the land which God had given them, they could never quite make up their minds to serve Him alone and to obey His commandments. It was always so much easier just to copy what other people did, especially the followers of the false God, Baal.

That was when Elijah, the prophet of the one true God, challenged them with the question, *'How long will you go limping with two different opinions?'* In other words, how long will you dither, unable to choose and make up your minds one way or the other? – *'If the Lord is God, follow Him; but if Baal, then follow him.'*

Elijah was telling his people to be strong, to have a will of their own, to make a choice. And that is something we must all learn to do.

If we are followers of the true God, then we will not be like 'King Very-Well-Then'. We will learn when it is right to say 'yes' and 'no', and to take a stand for the things that are important, no matter what anybody else around us is saying or doing. And, if we choose to serve the true God, many of the other choices of life will be so much easier, because our chief aim will always be to please Him.

◆ PRAYER –
Lord, help us not to be the kind of people who can never make up their minds on anything. Help us to be resolute in what we decide, and especially in Your service. In Jesus' name. Amen.

The
Confusing Signpost

◆ TEXT – John 14: 5 and 6
Thomas said, ' ... how can we know the way?'
Jesus said, 'I am the way ...'

SIGNPOSTS are such useful things, just as long as nobody tampers with them! That was what one of our Councils discovered some time ago. It happened when Bearsden and Milngavie District Council decided that a special sign should be placed at the exit of the railway station at Milngavie. That is the starting point for the West Highland Way, and the aim of the sign was to direct travellers on the route they should follow.

The West Highland Way is a 95 mile route, along which travellers will walk for several days, taking them over the hills and through some of the most wonderful scenery in Scotland, all the way to Fort William. Chosen for its natural beauty, it passes places like Drymen, Balmaha, Rowardennan, Inversnaid, Loch Lomond, Crianlarich, Tyndrum, Bridge of Orchy, Rannoch Moor, Kinlochleven and Glencoe.

These were the places the walker should have found by following the sign outside Milngavie station. But the men who put the sign in place seemed either to have left out two of the screws which held it in place, or had failed to tighten them sufficiently, so that it was capable of being moved.

Now, boys and girls in Bearsden and Milngavie are not very different from children anywhere else. In no time at all they had discovered that the sign had a weakness. Soon they had performed the prank of pointing it in the wrong direction. That meant that walkers getting off the train at Milngavie and following the direction in which the sign was now pointing, instead of following a route which should have taken them to Fort William, were now heading for places like Torrance and Kirkintilloch and Strathblane.

Torrance, Kirkintilloch and Strathblane are all very fine places, and all of them are worth a visit. But none of them is the place where you want to be if your intention is to walk the West Highland Way. In fact, to be re-routed so that you make a detour to these places is a waste of time, as many unsuspecting travellers were to discover. The sign which had been erected to help them only served to confuse.

That might make us ask the question whether there is a signpost that can guide us on the right way in life. Above all, is there a sign which is true and trustworthy? One of the disciples, a man called Thomas, once asked Jesus that very question: *'How can we know the way?'* The answer Jesus gave was: *'I am the way.'*

That means, if we follow Jesus we will never take the wrong way. Above all, we will never waste our time looking for the best things in life by travelling in the wrong direction.

◆ PRAYER –
Lord Jesus Christ, all through our lives help us to follow You Who are the way, and bring us in safety to our journey's end. Amen.

The
Windy City

◆ TEXT – Matthew 6: 7-8
'And in praying do not heap up empty phrases as the Gentiles do; for they think that they will be heard for their many words. Do not be like them, for Your Father knows what you need before you ask Him.'

HAVE you ever heard of the 'Windy City'? In one of the great musical films, 'Calamity Jane', there is a song which has the words:

Just blew in from the Windy City;
The Windy City is mighty pretty
But it ain't got what we got.
No, siree!

I have never been to the place where Calamity Jane stayed, so I have no way of knowing whether it has more to offer than the 'Windy City' or not, but one thing I do know is that those who visit the 'Windy City' soon discover that it is indeed a 'mighty pretty' place.

The 'Windy City' is the name given to Chicago. Chicago is a famous city in the northern part of the United States of America. It is in the state of Illinois, and it is situated at the south west end of one of the Great Lakes called Lake Michigan.

Chicago is well known for lots of reasons. It is the second largest city in America. Like London, much of it was rebuilt after a great fire in 1871 so that now, with its huge skyscrapers, it is a very attractive place.

Chicago has some wonderful buildings. It has one building which contains stones from countries all over the world, including a stone from our own Parliament buildings and another from the Pyramids of Egypt.

Chicago also has the second tallest building in the world. It is called the Sears Tower which is 110 storeys high. From the top, on a clear day, you can see four different states of the United States of America – a very long way indeed!

Chicago too has plenty to interest the visitors – a fine art gallery, a planetarium, a concert hall, and, down by the shore of Lake Michigan, a yachting marina and a very fine pier.

But it is a windy city, and when you are walking downtown in Chicago you can feel the wind coming up from the lakeshore and blowing along the tall, skyscraper buildings as though through a funnel.

Most people think that is why it is called the 'Windy City', but it is not the real reason for the name. Chicago was called the 'Windy City' just because at one time it had politicians who loved the sound of their own voices and made long-winded speeches. That is where the name comes from – a crowd of windbags – and ever since it has been known as the 'Windy City'.

Few people enjoy long-winded speeches, whether they are made by politicians in the Senate or ministers in their churches. In fact, Jesus once had something to say about long-winded prayers. He spoke about people heaping up phrase after phrase, expecting that the more they had to say the more God would listen to them. Jesus assures us that God is not like that. God is like a father who knows our need even before we ask Him, and what He wants is our sincere and honest prayer, however brief it may be.

◆ PRAYER –
Lord God, as Jesus taught Your disciples to pray, so teach us by Your spirit, that our prayers and our worship must be genuine and sincere. In Jesus' name. Amen.

21

The
Doofer

◆ TEXT – Jeremiah 29: 13
'You will seek me and find me; when you seek me with all your heart.'

◆ VISUAL AID –
A remote control handset for a television receiver

DO you have an instrument like this in your house? [*Hold up remote control handset.*] What do we call something like this? .... That's right. It's a remote control for a television set. Well that, at any rate, is its official name. But other people, so I have discovered, have other names for it.

I have a friend who calls it a 'zapper'. That is a good name, because it describes the popping or zapping noise you hear when you change from one channel to another. But the name I like best is the name that my wife uses. She calls this thing a 'doofer', so that occasionally I am asked, 'Would you pass the *doofer*, please?'

The first time I heard my wife say this, I asked, 'Why do you call it a doofer?'

'Well,' she said in reply, 'it will *do for* you what you really ought to do for yourself.'

And that is quite true. When you want to change channels, it is always possible to get up and select your programme from the buttons on the television set; but it is much handier just to stay in a comfortable seat instead and press the channel number on the doofer. It is indeed a device to '*do for* you' what you are able to *do for* yourself.

What a wonderful world it would be if somebody were to invent a

22

multi-purpose 'doofer', one that could do anything that we wanted. I mean, just imagine a 'doofer' that would do our homework for us, or clean up our room for us, or hang up the clothes which we are too lazy to put in the wardrobe. Sometimes I would like a 'doofer' to prepare my services for me.

But there is a problem about that. What do you think it is? The problem is that if there were such a thing as a 'doofer' which could do for us whatever had to be done, then we would soon lose the ability to do things for ourselves. Our skills would disappear very quickly and we would grow incredibly lazy. So there are many things in life that we simply must do for ourselves.

Sometimes I come across people who have not learned that lesson. Some people think, for example, that faith comes from a 'doofer'. But that is not true. Faith does not work like that. We cannot switch it on when we need it, and turn it off when we feel no need of it. Even worse, some people think that God can be controlled with a 'doofer', because they imagine that they can do without Him whenever they want, and then summon Him just when it suits them as if by the push of a button. But that does not work either.

The Old Testament prophet once said, *'You will seek me and find me; when you seek me with all your heart'*. Jeremiah knew very well that faith is something we have to work at constantly, just as he also knew that we can only find God when we put all our heart into seeking for Him.

◆ PRAYER –
Lord, remind us that there are things which we must do for ourselves. Above all, help us to love You with all our heart and soul and might. In Jesus' name. Amen.

23

Boomerang
Christians

◆ TEXT – Mark 8: 35-36
'For whoever would save his life will lose it; and whoever loses his life for my sake and the gospel's will save it. For what does it profit a man, to gain the whole world and forfeit his life?'

◆ VISUAL AID –
A boomerang, authentic or imitation

CAN anyone tell me what this object in my hand is? [*Hold up the boomerang.*] Can you tell me what country it comes from? I'd like to tell you a sad story from a song which a man called Charlie Drake used to sing. [*If you have a tape of Charlie Drake singing, play it. Otherwise sing it or simply read the words.*]

My boomerang won't come back,
my boomerang won't come back.
> *I've waved and waved it all over the place.*
> *I've practiced till I was black in the face.*
> *I'm a great disgrace to the Aborigine race.*
My boomerang won't come back.

This sad little man found that whereas a boomerang was supposed to come back to you when you threw it, his would not. So he went and consulted a wise old man who gave him the answer, 'Son, if you want your boomerang to come back, then first you have to throw it'! His boomerang wouldn't come back because he had not thrown it in the first place. 'If you want your boomerang to come back, then first you have to throw it.'

That seems so simple, but so often we forget, as Christians, that this is also what Christianity is all about. That is why Jesus told his followers that they must be ready to give their lives in order to find them properly. It is when we give we find that we receive. If we give happiness to others, we get it back again. If we show kindness to others, we suddenly discover that other people are kind too.

Jesus did that himself. He came and gave his life for this world, but giving it away didn't end it. Giving his life away meant that he came alive again. But He could not have been raised to life unless he had first died.

The boomerang won't come back unless you throw it. You won't find happiness as a Christian unless you give it to others. You won't find love unless you show love to others. Let's try being boomerang Christians – giving, and then finding that we will receive.

◆ PRAYER –
Lord Jesus, as You gave Yourself for us, help us to know that it is in giving that we receive, in loving that we are loved, and in serving that we find peace. Amen.

Say
'Shibboleth'

◆ TEXT – Judges 12: 1-6

◆ VISUAL AID –
Sheet displaying the word 'SHIBBOLETH' (with removable first letter 'H')

IN the book of the Judges, there is the story of a battle which took place between the men from Gilead and the men from Ephraim.

The Gileadites won the battle and the people of Ephraim were trying to escape. In order to do that they had to cross a narrow bit of river. The people from Gilead weren't always very sure who was an Ephraimite and who was a Gileadite, so they asked everybody who came to the crossing place to say the word, 'shibboleth'! [*Display the word.*] But the people from Ephraim couldn't say the word 'shibboleth'. They couldn't pronounce it properly and they would say 'sibboleth!' [*Display the word with the first 'h' removed.*] Then the men from Gilead knew that the person came from Ephraim.

It is very like the difference between Scotland and England. They tell us that people from England cannot say, 'It's a braw bricht moonlicht nicht the nicht'. They do not pronounce the words like that. So you should be able to tell a person from England from a person from Scotland. A person from England finds it very hard to say, 'It's a braw bricht moonlicht nicht the nicht'.

Christians, in the early days of the Church, were asked to say something that they couldn't say either. They lived in the great Roman Empire, and in order to be sure that all its citizens were loyal, there was a rule in the Roman Empire that each person had to go to a temple once a year and

26

take an oath saying 'Caesar is Lord'. But Christians believed that Jesus was their Lord, and they refused to say 'Caesar is Lord'.

The Romans decided that those who would not say 'Caesar is Lord' should be treated as traitors, and many of them were put in prison, while others were even put to death. What brave Christian people they were who would only say 'Jesus is Lord'.

As Christian people today, we have to keep on saying 'Jesus is Lord'. When people try to persuade us to allow other things to rule our lives, we have got to keep saying 'Jesus is Lord. We only obey him'. When people try to tempt us to do things that are wrong, we have got to say 'Jesus is our Lord. We only do what he wants us to do'.

The Ephraimites couldn't say, 'shibboleth'. The English can't say, 'it's a braw bri<u>ch</u>t moonli<u>ch</u>t ni<u>ch</u>t the ni<u>ch</u>t'. So, as Christians, we have to learn not to say that anyone is Lord *except* Jesus.

◆ PRAYER –
O God, You have told us that we should have no other Gods before You. Help us to follow Jesus and Him alone, so that we may truly worship You as our God. Amen.

The
Existence of God

◆ TEXT – John 3: 8 (Revised English Bible)
'The wind blows where it wills; you hear the sound of it, but you do not know where it comes from or where it is going.'

◆ VISUAL AID – An emu or some sort of hand puppet; and a balloon

[*This children's talk is best done if someone can be secreted in the pulpit <u>before</u> the children come into church. The minister begins his children's address, the content of which is not important, but while he is speaking the head of the emu should appear from the pulpit. The children will most likely draw your attention to it, but you must pretend not to have seen it, and deny the fact that it has happened, or that there is anything there at all.*

As you continue the talk, the emu or puppet appears again, this time clutching a balloon which it drops from the pulpit. The children will, no doubt, draw your attention to this as well. They will tell you that the puppet has dropped a balloon. One of them may then be asked to come forward and pick the balloon up to show you, thus proving that an emu has indeed appeared and dropped a balloon. The real address now continues ...]

OKAY, boys and girls, I'm convinced. There *must* be an emu in the pulpit. I didn't believe you at first because I hadn't seen it. But now you've shown me that it has actually done something. It has dropped a balloon from the pulpit – I can't argue with that because *there is a balloon*. You have shown me it.

You know, sometimes people will tell you that there isn't a God. They can't see God, so they say that He cannot be there. And maybe

28

you argue with them. Maybe you tell them that there *is* a God and they don't believe you. But once you can show them something that God has done, then they may believe you. I didn't see the emu, but you did. I didn't believe you, but when you showed me the balloon that it had dropped, I had to believe you.

If people see what God has done for us, they will come to believe in Him. If they see that God makes us better people, happier people, kinder people, then they will realise that God is there in this world, helping, doing things, guiding people. You can't see God, but when you see the things that He has done, when you see the people He has helped, when you see how He has changed people, then you will believe that God is there, alive and active in this world.

[If you consider it fitting, the morning can be made more memorable for the children if, during the singing of the children's hymn, the emu or puppet appears again clutching a hymnbook and seeming to join in the singing of the hymn.]

◆ PRAYER –
O God our Father, help us to see You in the things that happen in the world, to see You in the love of other people, to see You in the beauty and the wonder of this Universe, and, above all, to see You in the life of Jesus. Amen.

On
Your own

- ◆ OCCASION – Sunday after Ascension

- ◆ TEXT – Matthew 28: 19-20
  'Go therefore and make disciples of all nations, baptizing them in the name of the Father and of the Son and of the Holy Spirit, teaching them to observe all that I have commanded you; and lo, I am with you always, to the close of the age.'

- ◆ VISUAL AID – A pair of swimming armbands

WHAT would you use this pair of swimming armbands for? How would they help you to swim or to float?

In the past, before these were used, sometimes people would learn to float in water by having a friend support them, their hand held under their back so that they did not sink. It was a very pleasant feeling to be lying there floating on the water. But then, when you realised that the person's hand was no longer there, you panicked, and your legs started to thrash about and you swallowed gallons of water – at least you felt that you did! It was all right while the supporting hand was there helping you to float. But when you realised that it was no longer there, and that you were on your own, then you became frightened, thinking that you were going to sink.

It was the same when you were learning to ride a bicycle. Anyone who learned to ride a bicycle, before 'stabilisers' had been invented, would have their mum or dad walk or run alongside them holding on to the back of the saddle and making sure that the bike did not fall over.

And, once again, you would be going along quite happily until you suddenly realised that they were no longer holding on to the back of the bike. You were on your own. Then you would start to panic a wee bit, and wobble a wee bit, and, unless the person caught the back of the saddle again, you might even have fallen off. It was all right while you thought that there was someone with you, but when you realised that you were on your own it was a bit frightening.

This is the Sunday when we remember that Jesus left his disciples 'on their own'. They were not going to see Him any more, although He promised that He would be with them just the same. It must have been very frightening for these followers of Jesus when they knew that He wasn't there any more for them to watch, to listen to, and to ask for advice. Sometimes they had been quite brave and courageous when they knew that He was with them, but the thought that He wouldn't be there must have been very frightening indeed.

However Jesus gave them a promise that, although they could no longer see Him, He would be with them to give them the words they needed to speak and the strength they needed to do the things that He wanted them to do. His promise was, 'I am with you always to the end of time'.

Jesus promised to be with us too. He asks us to do all sorts of things for His sake. Sometimes we get quite frightened because we feel that we are on our own. When others laugh at us, when others want to do things that we think we shouldn't do, we must remember that He is with us even to the end of time and will never leave us.

◆ PRAYER –
O God, our Father, You have promised us in Jesus Christ that You will be with us even to the end of time. Help us, therefore, never to be afraid or lonely or downhearted, because You are with us to help us, to support us, and will never leave us. Amen.

Spreading
the Word

◆ TEXT – Matthew 13: 4-9

◆ VISUAL AID – A dandelion head in seed, or a sycamore seed

AT the very beginning of the Bible we are told that when the world began, God gave us plants that bear seed, every tree bearing fruit that yields seed. This is the way in which plants keep alive. They produce seed, and that seed scatters, and it creates more plants and trees.

Let's try an experiment this morning. Let's see how seeds scatter. [*Either throw from the pulpit some sycamore seeds yourself, or blow the seeds from the top of a dandelion head; or allow children to do this either from the pulpit or the gallery. Point out how the sycamore seeds flutter down with a propeller-like movement, or how the dandelion seeds fall like tiny parachutes.*]

So now you see what a wonderful way God has designed these plants. They are formed so that the seeds can fly for miles, with the wind blowing them. They then plant themselves somewhere else, spreading new sycamore trees or dandelions (which might not be very popular with your mums and dads in their garden)!

This is how God's kingdom grows too. Seed is sown and things grow from it. The message Jesus gave his friends was taken by them through the countryside where they lived. The Bible also tells us how the message of Christianity was spread through Asia Minor into Europe.

We know ourselves of people who have gone from our land, taking the message of Christianity to other places. And we know how people from other countries come to us with new and lively messages about the Christian gospel which we need to hear as well. This is how the word of

God spreads. This is how the Christian Church grows. This is how the gospel of Jesus finds root in the hearts and minds of people.

We can sow this sort of seed for Jesus. By our words, by helping and loving people, by forgiving and caring for people, we can sow the seeds of Jesus' love. And sometimes you'll be surprised just how much of an effect what you say and do can have on others; how what you do and say can help others – how you can plant the seeds of God's love in other people.

◆ PRAYER –
Lord Jesus, You sent Your disciples to take the message of God's love to all people. Use us also to spread Your kingdom, to show Your love, and to help other people to follow You. Amen.

Sing of
the Lord's Goodness

◆ TEXT – Acts 16: 25
'... about midnight Paul and Silas were praying and singing hymns to God, and the prisoners were listening to them.'

HAVE you been on any trips recently? Maybe you have been on a school trip to some place of interest, or maybe on an outing to a pantomime? Or maybe your Sunday School arranged a trip?

When children go on a trip by bus they usually sing songs. Do you do that? What kind of songs do you sing? I've heard boys and girls on a trip singing these words loud and clear:

The back of the bus they cannae sing,
They cannae sing, they cannae sing.
The back of the bus they cannae sing,
They cannae sing for peanuts.

(TUNE: 'Here we go round the Mulberry Bush')

The great thing about that song is that it is sung louder than anything else. The front of the bus and the back of the bus try to drown each other out with the words. In fact I have never heard anything that is sung louder than that, as the front of the bus and the back of the bus try to prove the point! Maybe we could improve the singing in the church by having a few rounds of

The back of the church they cannae sing,
They cannae sing for peanuts.

34

The strange thing is, of course, that this is a song that says unkind things about other people. Isn't it funny that the song we sing loudest is one that is slagging other people?

Very often at football matches and similar events the songs that are sung loudest are the songs against the other team.

At one time Paul and his friend Silas were put in prison in Philippi. They were locked up by the jailor, having been arrested by the Roman soldiers. At midnight they started to sing. I wonder what they were singing? Do you think it might have been something like

If you hate the Roman soldiers clap your hands ...

(TUNE: 'She'll be coming round the Mountains')

That's what you might have expected them to sing. The Roman soldiers, after all, had locked them away. It wasn't fair and it wasn't right! But that wasn't what they were singing at all. They were singing praises to God. Even though things weren't going very well, they still sang praise to God – hymns of happiness.

Wouldn't it be good if we could put as much effort into singing about the good things – the love of God, the goodness of Jesus – as we do into the nasty things we sing about each other? What God has done for us, and the way He loves us and helps us, is something really worth singing about – and singing loudly!

◆ PRAYER –
We ask You, Lord, to give us hands to serve You, hearts to love You, and voices to praise You, for all that You have done for us and given to us. Amen.

The
Clock Change

◆ TEXT – Romans 12: 2
*'Do not be conformed to this world but be transformed by the renewal of
your mind, that you may prove what is the will of God, what is good and
acceptable and perfect.'*

◆ VISUAL AID – A picture of a clock at the wrong time
(either one hour slow or fast, as the occasion demands)

THIS is the day on which people sometimes arrive an hour too early
[or *an hour too late*] for church. Why is that? It is because the clock has
changed. Last night everyone should have put their clocks one hour
forward [or *backwards*] because it's the beginning [or *the end*] of British
Summer Time.

Just imagine what it would be like if you decided that you were
going to be different. Imagine deciding that you weren't going to change
the clock. I've heard of people who refused to do so in small country
places. They just carried on using the clock as it was. They talked about
the time that they were going by as 'God's time', and British Summer
Time as 'Fool's time'.

What would happen if you did that? You would be an hour too early
[or *too late*] for school. If you were going to a football match you would
have to wait for an hour before the game started [or *arrive just after
half time*]. If you were invited to a party, you would be late [or *early*]. It
wouldn't be a very sensible thing to do.

However, there are some times when we have to be different and
not be afraid to be different. People are always wanting us to be the

36

same as them, to do the things that they do. But quite often, because we are Christians, we have to refuse to do the things that some other people do, and we've got to do things that they won't do. We try to follow Jesus and we try to do the things He showed us, and follow His example, and be like Him.

Sometimes, of course, people can't understand why we are different, and we've got to be able to tell them that it is because we follow Jesus.

There was once an American writer called Henry James Thoreau who was so unhappy about the life that people were living that he went away to live on his own, to think things out. Eventually he wrote a book, and in it these words are found: 'If a man does not keep pace with his companions, perhaps it is because he hears a different drummer. Let him step to the music he hears, however measured or far away.'

Thoreau heard a different drummer and marched to a different beat, and that's what Christians have to do. We have to hear what Jesus asks us to do and to obey Him and follow Him. That often means that we will be different from everyone else. It often means that we won't do the same things as others do. But we are listening to Jesus. We are obeying Him. He is the drummer, and we are marching to the beat of His drum.

◆ PRAYER –
Lord Jesus, give us the courage to follow You and to do the things You want us to do, and never to be afraid of what others think of us, or say of us. Amen.

The
Bible Diary

◆ TEXT – Psalm 103: 1-3
'Bless the Lord, O my Soul;
and all that is within me,
bless His holy name!
Bless the Lord, O my soul,
and forget not all His benefits,
who forgives all your iniquity,
who heals all your diseases.'

◆ VISUAL AID – a diary

BOYS and girls, what kind of book is this in my hand? [*Hold up diary.*]
That's right. It's a diary. Do any of you keep a diary? What sort of things
do you write in it?

This diary, if I look back before today's date, tells me the things that
I have done during the past year. [*List some examples.*] If I look forward,
after today's date, it tells me all the things that I am going to have to
do this week, and the next week, and the week after that. [*List more
examples.*]

In a diary you write down what you have done or what you are
going to do. When you read it later on, it reminds you what you have
already done, and also allows you to look forward to see the things that
you are going to do.

I think the diary is very like the Bible that is brought in at the beginning of the service. It does two things. First, when we read the Bible,
we see what God has done in the past. We see how God led the Jewish

people, chose them and guided them to become a great nation. We see how He helped them, corrected them, how He saved and restored them when they went astray. We also read in our Bible what Jesus did, how He called His friends to help and serve Him, how He helped people and healed people, how He lived and suffered and died for us. So the Bible tells us very much what has happened in the past, what God has done for this world and through Jesus.

The Bible also tells us what we have to do in the future, how we have to respond to all God's goodness and love. It tells us the things we should do for other people, to help them, to show love for them, to care for them. It shows how we have to tell others about God's love, show them by our love for them how much God loves us. The Bible tells us how we ought to live our lives, the kind of people we should try to be. And it also tells us what God will do for us in the future – how He will help us, guide us, lead us and forgive us.

Whenever the Church Officer brings the Bible into the church on a Sunday morning, it is like our diary telling us what God has done for us in the past, of what He will do for us in the future, and of the things we have to do to be loving and faithful disciples of Jesus.

◆ PRAYER –
O God, whenever we read Your Bible, open our eyes to see what You have done for us, and open our hearts to respond to Your love, and to do the things that You want us to do. Amen.

O'Grady
Says

◆ TEXT – John 13: 15

'For I have given you an example, that you should do as I have done to you.'

THIS morning, boys and girls, we are going to begin with a game. [*Here introduce the well known game, 'O'Grady Says', remembering that there are other versions of it with different names giving the commands. Explain that when O'Grady gives a command – such as O'Grady says 'stand up' – then you all stand. If, on the other hand, a command is given without O'Grady saying it, such as 'sit down', then you do not do it.*

The game can be played with the elimination of those who fail to obey the commands correctly. So, for example, those who 'stand up' when O'Grady hasn't given the command, would be 'out'. Those who 'sit down' when O'Grady has given the order, remain 'in'. Even within the confines of a church pew, such commands as 'raise your hands', 'shut your eyes', 'clench your fists', 'lift your hymnbooks', can be managed quite easily.

At the end of the game, if everyone is out, or a number are out, it should be explained that we could always have another game, so that all the children would be 'in' and could start again. After the game, the talk proceeds ...]

That was fun, boys and girls, wasn't it? Being a Christian is very much like that game. Jesus said, *'I have given you an example that you should do as I have done to you'*. Following Jesus means doing what Jesus wants us to do. Being a Christian also involves not doing the things that Jesus doesn't tell us to do. So, when we are going to do anything, we should ask ourselves, 'Does Jesus want me to do this?' If Jesus says 'do it', then we do it. If Jesus says 'don't do it', then we do not do it. We have to follow His example and do as He does. We have to do what He wants us to do. That means that just as He helped other people, so we have to help them. Just as He showed love and forgiveness to others, so we have to show love and forgiveness too. Just as He never did anything to hurt anyone, so we shouldn't do anything to hurt anyone.

If you did the wrong thing when we were playing 'O'Grady Says', then you were 'out'. You made a mistake. Quite often we make mistakes in the Christian life too. We do the wrong things. We don't follow Jesus. We don't obey His commands. But that doesn't put us 'out' forever. He is willing to forgive us and to let us start again. He is willing to give us a new start, so that we can try again as his followers, doing only the things that He wants us to do.

◆ PRAYER –
We thank You, God, for giving Jesus to be our example. Help us to follow Him by trying to do the things He taught us to do and showing the love He had for us. We ask this for his sake. Amen.

The
Eye Chart

◆ TEXT – 2 Kings 6: 17
   '… open his eyes that he may see.'

◆ VISUAL AID –
   The letters of the text 2 Kings 6: 17, printed on a card in the form of an optician's eye chart, the letters becoming progressively smaller

HAVE you ever had your eyes tested by an optician or by the school doctor? When he is testing your eyes, the optician will use something like this. This is an eye chart. As you can see, it is simply a card containing letters of the alphabet and the letters get smaller and smaller on each line down. The optician asks you to read the letters, and, by noting which ones you misread, he will make further tests, and then prescribe glasses if you should need them.

Maybe someone would like to come out and read this chart for me this morning, letter by letter. First you have to cover one eye. Now read the letters one by one. Now cover the other eye, and try it again.

Well done. That was a good effort. But did you notice the words which are actually formed by these letters? Let's look at the chart again. If you read the letters together you discover that they make up these words – 'Open his eyes that he may see.' It's quite obvious isn't it, now that it has been pointed out?

The trouble is that sometimes we look, but do not truly see.

These words, *'Open his eyes that he may see'*, were originally a prayer. It was spoken by a man called Elisha, a prophet whom we read about in the Old Testament. Elisha was being pursued by a huge army of the

42

Assyrians. His young servant looked out one morning and, seeing a great host of their warriors surrounding them, was terrified, and he cried out, 'Alas, my Master! What shall we do?' It was then that Elisha prayed the words, 'Lord ... open his eyes that he may see'.

What Elisha wanted the young man to see and to understand was that neither of them had reason to fear – because God was on their side. Indeed, the Bible story goes on to tell us that both Elisha and the young man, who was his servant, were delivered from danger.

'Lord ... open our eyes that we may see.' That is a prayer that all of us should pray when we are anxious, afraid, or in any kind of trouble. Then, like the young man of Dothan, when we remember that God is on our side, we will be able to face our difficulties with hope and confidence and a quiet heart.

◆ PRAYER –
Lord God, help us never to forget that You are a very present help in trouble. Open our eyes that we may see, and realising Your presence, face our difficulties unafraid. Amen.

Illuminations

◆ TEXT – Matthew 5: 14
'You are the light of the world.'

MANY seaside towns have what are called 'illuminations'. These are fancy-coloured lights put together in a display which helps to brighten the late summer and autumn evenings. The town of Blackpool is perhaps the best known for its display of lights. There, every year, a celebrity is specially invited to press a switch which lights up a million coloured light bulbs along the sea front.

Another holiday town which has 'illuminations' is Bournemouth. Part of the display there is very unusual. Near the sea front is a park, and all around the edge of this park, wooden frames have been erected, and on these frames thousands of little glass jars are hung. The jars are so arranged that they form the outline of such items as a windmill, a lighthouse, a ship, a flower, a bird or a butterfly. Sometimes people who are visiting Bournemouth for the first time can be seen looking into these glass jars, and they are surprised to discover that they contain, not an electric light bulb, but a small candle.

On certain evenings in late summer, hundreds of special lighters are given out to holidaymakers, who can then go and light one of the candles. It is exciting to watch as children of all ages, together with their parents, grandparents, aunts and uncles, make their way around the park spreading the light. So, gradually, the shapes all come to life, and there is a feeling of achievement as the darkness is dispelled by the light of thousands of little flames, everyone playing a part in creating the display.

One of our favourite hymns is 'Jesus bids us shine', and part of it contains the words, 'in this world is darkness'. The hymnwriter was reminding us that there are many things in the world which make people sad – like selfishness, greed, jealousy and unkindness.

That's why some people wish that we could simply press a switch and change the world, making it a brighter place – just as someone presses a switch in Blackpool lighting up the sea front.

The fact is, however, that our world will only become brighter and cheerier when each of us plays a part in making it like that. Every one of us can help to bring the light of understanding, friendship, kindness and tolerance to our corner of the world. Only then will the darkness be dispelled. That's why Jesus told his followers, *'You are the light of the world'*. Today, too, 'Jesus bids us shine'.

◆ PRAYER –
Lord Jesus Christ, wherever there is darkness, help us to shine with a light that helps others to see the way. Amen.

The
False Face

◆ OCCASION – Hallowe'en

◆ TEXT – Luke 12: 56
  'You hypocrites!'

◆ VISUAL AID –
  A false face or mask

LAST night was All Hallows' Eve or, as we usually call it, 'Hallowe'en'. Maybe sometime last week you attended a Hallowe'en party and put on fancy dress for the occasion. Maybe your costume also involved wearing one of these [*hold up the mask*] – a false face.

Hallowe'en is probably the only time that we wear a false face, but in parts of India certain workers are actually encouraged to wear a false face every day as they go to work. These men work in the forests of West Bengal.

In that area the fearsome Sundarban tiger often attacks workers as they go about their duties in the forest, so the Indian government had to find a solution to the problem. One way would have been to hunt and kill the tigers, but nobody wanted that. So another plan was put into operation. Noting that this tiger only attacked humans from behind, the authorities issued the workers with rubber face masks, and they were told to wear them, not over their faces, but on the back of their heads. Happily, since the experiment began in 1987, not one single worker who has worn a mask has been attacked.

Here in our country there are no wild tigers, so people do not need to wear false faces every day. Yet there are some people who seem to do that, even if it is not Hallowe'en. These are people who pretend to be what they are not. They appear to be friendly and kind and considerate, when really they are mean and nasty and selfish.

In the gospels we read of how Jesus met people like that and how they made Him very angry. He had a word for them – He called them 'hypocrites', and the word originally meant someone who play-acts. Jesus said that His followers should not be like people who were acting a part. They were to be honest and sincere in all that they said and did.

So let's make sure that we keep our false face for Hallowe'en only, and on all the other days of the year, be what we seem.

◆ PRAYER –
Lord Jesus, today and everyday, help us to be true to ourselves, to others and to You. For Your love's sake. Amen.

The
White Rhino

◆ TEXT – Hebrews 13: 18 (Authorised Version)
'... have a good conscience ... in all things.'

WHAT colour is a White Rhino? The name suggests that it must be white, or at least *nearly* white. But White Rhinos, in fact, are a pale grey colour. So why are they called 'white'?

The name came about because of a misunderstanding. The first Europeans to settle in the southern areas of the African continent were Dutch, and it was the Dutch people who named one species of rhinoceros the *'weit* rhino'. *Weit* is the Dutch word for 'wide' – and they called that type of rhino the 'weit rhino' because of its wide, almost square, upper lip and muzzle. Later, when English colonists arrived, they mistook the Dutch word *weit* for the English word 'white', and so the name of 'White Rhino' stuck.

The rhino is a very large animal with a reputation for its short temper. It is liable to charge anyone or anything which comes too close. Yet the strange thing is that these great beasts tolerate the company of a little bird called the Oxteker. These little brown birds perch on the rhino's back, feeding on insects which settle on the animal's hide.

This strange arrangement is of benefit both to the rhino and the oxteker – the oxteker has found a source of food, while the rhino, whose eyesight is very poor, relies on the oxteker which, from its high vantage point, is able to warn of approaching danger. The oxteker does this by making a hissing sound and so providing an early warning system to the rhino.

Unlike the 'White Rhino' we do not have a little bird perched on our shoulder to warn of danger, but all of us have a kind of 'early warning system' which operates whenever we are in danger of doing wrong. It is called our conscience and its warning is unmistakable.

Do you remember in the film 'Pinnochio', that little Jiminy Cricket sang a song called 'Always let your conscience be your guide'.

We too should 'always let our conscience be our guide'. Whenever we are in danger of doing or saying something which is wrong or harmful to other people, we should stop and listen to our 'early warning system' which gives us no peace until the danger is over. That is why one of the New Testament letters offers advice which is as wise for us today as it was for those who first read it – *'have a good conscience … in all things'*.

◆ PRAYER –
Lord God, we give You thanks for all the ways in which You speak to us, and especially today we thank You for the voice of conscience. Help us always to listen to it, and, having listened, to obey it, that in all things we may learn to live as You would have us live. In Jesus' name. Amen.

The
Gift of Joy

◆ TEXT – Galatians 5: 22
'... the fruit of the Spirit is ... joy.'

◆ VISUAL AID –
A porcelain figure of a child by Hummel

THIS morning, boys and girls, I have a little girl with me. In fact she is so small that she can fit into my pocket. [*Produce figurine.*]

Most of you will have seen a little china figure like this. You may even have one like it at home. Figures like this, which are made in a factory in Germany, are sold in countries all over the world. They are called Hummel figures and there is a whole series of them. All depict jolly little children doing the things that jolly little children enjoy doing. So perhaps it is not surprising that there are people who collect as many of these as they can. What may surprise you, however, is that they owe their existence to the drawings of a nun whose name was Sister Maria Innocentia Hummel.

Most people, when they think of nuns, imagine rather solemn individuals dressed in sombre black clothes. But Sister Maria was not like that at all. Born in 1909, she was the third daughter of Adolf and Victoria Hummel, who lived in the German town of Massing. Her own name was Bertha. Her mother once said, 'By the time Bertha was three, we knew she was an exceptionally gifted child. She would often sit by the window, pencil in hand, day dreaming and scribbling. When she went to school, she spent more time drawing than paying attention to what was going on in class'.

50

After studying art in Munich, Bertha entered a convent of the Franciscan order of sisters, taking the name of Sister Maria Innocentia. There her gentle sense of fun made her popular with the other sisters and her happy laughter was often heard ringing round the corridors. There too she was able to continue her passion for drawing, and it was at this time that she produced her loveable sketches of children.

In 1934 a porcelain factory owner called Franz Goebel became aware of Sister Maria's drawings, and he persuaded her to have little china figures made from them. That is how the now world-famous Hummel figures came to exist.

Sister Maria herself died in 1946, but her name and her joy and her love of life continue to be remembered in these china figures which are so popular.

Lots of people still imagine that followers of Jesus must be solemn and serious. Nothing could be further from the truth, because our faith is about the good news of God's love for us which we see in Jesus. At His birth, the angel said, 'I bring you good news of a great joy'. Before He left them, Jesus told His disciples that he wanted his 'joy to remain in them', and Paul tells us that *the fruit of the Spirit is ... joy*.

Indeed, when the Roman Catholic Church is considering making someone a saint, and that person's life is being examined, one of the qualities which the examiners look for is 'heroic joy'. That is to say, the saint had not only to be a good and godly person, but a joyful one.

Joy is one of the great Christian graces. So, as we grow, let us ask God to give us the precious gift of the joyful heart.

◆ PRAYER –
Lord Jesus, we thank You that You have shown us the love that God has for us. Help us, sure of that love, to possess the joy that no one can take away from us. For Your love's sake. Amen.

Bifocal
Vision

◆ OCCASION – Christian Aid Week

◆ TEXT 1 – Psalm 103: 2
  'Bless the Lord, O my soul,
      and forget not all his benefits.'
  TEXT 2 – Psalm 41: 1
  'Blessed is he who considers the poor!'

◆ VISUAL AID – A pair of bifocal glasses or spectacles

BOYS and girls, if you look round the congregation this morning, you will see that a great many of the people in church are wearing glasses. These glasses or spectacles will be quite different. They will vary, not just in the shape and the colour of the frames, but also in the size and the thickness of the lenses.

Some people need glasses to help them see things which are far away, although they are able to see things which are close at hand perfectly well. Others need glasses to help them see things which are close at hand, although they are able to see things which are far away perfectly well. But some people have been prescribed two pairs of specs – one pair for seeing things close at hand and another pair for seeing things far away. The trouble about needing two pairs is that you have to change them often through the day, depending on whether what you are looking at is close at hand or far away.

There is a way to overcome this problem. It is by wearing glasses like this pair which I have in my hand. These have two lenses in one.

They are known as 'bifocals' and they are easy to recognise, because they have a little half moon shaped lens at the bottom of each full lens. By using 'bifocals', a person looks straight ahead through the full lens for distance, while, when he or she wants to look at things which are close up, he simply looks down through the little half moon lens.

Sometimes I think we all need bifocal vision, if we are to live life well. But the strange thing is that, sometimes, even people who don't need glasses at all don't possess this vision.

How many there are, on the one hand, who fail to see and appreciate what is close at hand and all around them. Because of this they never seem to be thankful for all the blessings we enjoy in this rich and prosperous country in which we live. Here all of us have enough to eat. We have clean drinking water when we turn on a tap in our homes. If we fall ill we can easily call on a doctor, and, if necessary, be admitted to a hospital to be cared for. All this and more we enjoy every day. Yet many people seem unable to see these things and be grateful for them.

And how many more there are, on the other hand, who fail to see what is far away. These are people who never spare a thought for the poor and hungry in other countries, who never consider that there are men and women and boys and girls in the world who do not have enough to eat or clean water to drink, who forget that there are places where there are few doctors to care for the sick.

This coming week is Christian Aid Week. During it we are asked to give money to help the poor in many parts of the world. This is a time to use 'bifocal vision'. When we do that, we will appreciate the blessings near at hand which we enjoy day by day, and, like the Psalmist, we will say, *'Bless the Lord, O my soul, and forget not all his benefits'*. But, at the same time, we will look to the distance, thinking about those who have little. Then we will give all that we can to enable them to create a better life for themselves, remembering that *'Blessed is he who considers the poor!'*

◆ PRAYER –
Lord God, as we live, teach us to be grateful for all that we have been given, and give us eyes to see those who are in need and the will to do what we can to help. In Jesus' name. Amen.

53

Snowflakes

◆ TEXT – 1 Peter 5: 7
   ' … for he cares about you.'

WHAT colour is a snowflake? I think most of us would say that it is white. That's the obvious answer. But just for a few minutes, this morning, let's think about snowflakes.

Snow, as you will know, is frozen water. High up in the atmosphere, tiny droplets of water freeze to become ice crystals, and, as they form, they gather around them a speck of dust. Then, when a cluster of these crystals is large enough, it begins to float to the ground and we call it a snowflake.

Did you know that, in the past, coloured snow has actually fallen in parts of the world? Indeed, as recently as March 1991, yellow snow fell in parts of Finland and Sweden. It is believed to have happened because there was yellow pollen dust in the atmosphere at the time when the ice crystals were formed. That is why I began with the question, 'What colour is a snowflake?'

To be accurate, a snowflake is colourless. Just like the water from which it is formed, it has no real colour, and we all know from experience that if you allow a snowflake to melt on your hand it will simply return to colourless water. So why then do we normally see it as white? The answer is that the tiny ice crystals which form a snowflake have many different surfaces which reflect light, and our eyes see this as white light.

So, all in all, snowflakes are a very beautiful and wonderful part of God's world. They always have three or six sides, and the scientists tell us that of all the millions of snowflakes which are formed and float down to earth, no two are ever identical. Each has its own beauty, because snowflakes have a never-ending variety of shapes and sizes.

I think that is wonderful.

But just as wonderful as the snowflake is the fact that, of all the millions of people in this world, no two are identical. Even identical twins are not really *identical*. They have, for example, different finger prints, and there are differences in their eyes.

This means, boys and girls, that of the millions of people who have ever lived, and of all those who will be born in the future, not one will be exactly like you. Each of you is unique. Each of you has your own beauty. So never waste your time or energy being envious of someone else, wishing that you could look like them or be like them. Be glad of who you are, for there will only ever be one of you. And each of us, as we are, is special to God who, as the writer of 1 Peter tells us, *'cares about'* us.

◆ PRAYER –
Lord God, we thank You for the wonderful world in which we live. We thank You for making us as we are. Above all, we thank You, that You love every one of us. Help us to love You, as You have first loved us. In Jesus' name. Amen.

Safe
Hands

◆ TEXT – Psalm 37: 23-24 (Revised English Bible)
   'It is the Lord who directs a person's steps.
      He holds him firm and approves of his conduct.
   Though he may fall, he will not go headlong,
      for the Lord grasps him by the hand.'

I WONDER if any of the girls in church this morning attend dancing classes? If you do, then perhaps as part of your costume you will wear a 'leotard'. Most people know that a leotard is a tight-fitting garment, rather like a swimming costume, except it has sleeves and it is usually worn with tights. But not everyone knows the story of where the name comes from.

The costume takes its name from a French acrobat called Jules Leotard. He was the man who designed the flying trapeze. Until his time, acrobats performed their twists and turns on a fixed bar. Leotard, however, came up with the idea of suspending the bar from two ropes attached to the ceiling in his father's gymnasium. In this way the bar could be used like a swing, allowing the acrobat far greater freedom. Indeed, Jules Leotard was able to perform such amazing feats on this new device that crowds flocked from all over Europe to see him, and it was of him that a song was written, describing him as 'the daring young man on the flying trapeze'.

Soon others took up his idea and developed it until, in time, trapeze 'flying', usually involving a whole troupe of acrobats, became the popular and truly daring circus act that we know today.

What an exciting thing it is to watch! High above the sawdust ring, a flyer will launch himself from a swinging bar, often completing two or perhaps even three somersaults in mid-air, before being caught in the sure grasp of a person known as the 'catcher'. Over and over, the flyers perform their stunts; and over and over, when they have finished, they are held by the 'catcher'.

To those who know little of acrobatics or circuses, the 'catcher' appears the least daring of the flying trapeze group, because 'catching' is all that he seems to do. And yet he is a very important member of the team – the others rely totally on him. All the time that they are 'flying', he is watching every move. One mistake on his part could cause a flyer to fall and suffer serious injury. The rest of the team can perform with confidence, knowing that his strong and safe hands are ready to catch them and save them from falling.

In the Bible we read that the hands of God are safe and strong. The Psalmist tells us that *'it is the Lord who directs a person's steps. He holds him firm and approves of his conduct. Though he may fall, he will not go headlong, for the Lord grasps him by the hand'.*

It is a great thought that God is like this. That is why those who put their trust in Him can live their lives in confidence knowing that they are never beyond the grip of His hand.

◆ PRAYER –
  Lord God we give You thanks for Your love for us. Teach us to live securely in the knowledge that we cannot move beyond the bounds of Your care. In Jesus' name. Amen.

The Cathedral
of the Isles

◆ TEXT – Psalm 84: 10
'For a day in Thy courts is better than a thousand elsewhere.'

MILLPORT, on the the Island of Cumbrae in the Firth of Clyde, is a popular holiday spot for many people. Apart from walking its main street, looking at the shops, or enjoying its safe and sheltered bay with the inviting stretch of sand, a popular activity for holiday-makers and day-trippers alike is to cycle the flat coastal road which circuits the island, stretching for nine miles or so.

Some visitors to Millport who do this, however, are quite unaware that, just a few hundred yards inland, one of the most beautiful and unusual churches in Scotland is to be found on the island. Called the 'Cathedral of the Isles', it is the smallest cathedral in Great Britain and probably in Europe, for it barely seats one hundred worshippers, and attached to it is a college.

Inside the cathedral there are four beautiful stained-glass windows depicting saints of long ago. The floor is covered with coloured tiles and the ceiling is richly decorated. A simple wooden pulpit on one side of the church is balanced, on the other, by a large brass lectern in the form of an eagle with outspread wings. Every corner has something to catch the eye.

Most visitors, however, miss one very unusual feature, for high above the chancel, to the side of the altar, there is a small plain glass window. Hidden from the area of the main church it is difficult to see. On the other side of the window is the 'Infirmary', which is part of the adjoining college, and the window there was installed so that people who were ill and unable to attend the service could look down at it taking place.

It is always sad to have to miss worship, and while the builders of the cathedral in Millport were kind to spare a thought for the sick, nothing is quite the same as actually being present at church with other worshippers.

Some of the older members of our congregation are no longer able to be with us, and when I visit them they tell me how they will listen to a service on the radio or watch one on television, or join in the television programme 'Songs of Praise' in the evening. But many of them go on to say that while these programmes are enjoyable, none is ever quite the same as being in church with family or friends.

How wise we shall be then if, when we are young, we decide to be faithful in our attendance at worship. If we do that, then, like our older members and those who attended the Temple at Jerusalem, we will make the discovery that the Psalmist made, when he said *'a day in Thy courts is better than a thousand elsewhere'*.

◆ PRAYER –
Lord God, we thank You for Your Church, our mother in the faith, for its worship, its ministry and teaching. Help us so to play our part in its life that we will count Your worship our joy and delight. In Jesus' name. Amen.

Mind-reading

◆ TEXT – Psalm 139: 23-24
  'Search me, O God, and know my heart!
  Try me, and know my thoughts!
  And see if there be any wicked way in me,
  and lead me in the way everlasting!'

[*The mathematical trick described below will always result in the answer
'1089', no matter what numbers are chosen in the fashion detailed below.*]

BOYS and girls, can you tell me what a mind-reader does? .... That's
right, a mind-reader is a person who reads minds. A mind-reader is
someone who knows what you are thinking. I have been learning just a
little about mind-reading, and I thought I might try it out on you this
morning. In fact, *I know* what some of you are thinking right now –
you're thinking that I won't be able to do it!

Well, let's give it a try anyway! I want each of you to think of a
number. No, don't shout it out! Don't tell me what it is! Just keep it to
yourself, concentrate on it very hard, and, as I come along the pew, I'll
write down the numbers that are coming across most strongly from
your minds to mine. [*Move along the pew.*] My goodness, there *are* quite
a few numbers coming across very strongly, so I'm going to write them
down on this piece of card. [*Concealing it from the children, write down
the number 1089 on a large piece of card, and give it to someone to keep
hidden, or place it down nearby.*]

Now, I need a little help. I wonder if you can give me a number
between 1 and 3 .... Now, somebody else give me a number between

4 and 6 …….. Now somebody give me a number between 7 and 9 ……..
[*Write these numbers down so that the children can read them. As an example we might have the numbers 3, 6, and 8.*]

Now, just for a minute I want to play around with these numbers. The numbers you chose were 3, 6 and 8. So I'm going to reverse these, and then take the smaller number from the larger. That is 863 minus 368 which equals 495. Now I'm going to reverse that number and add the two numbers together. So we get 594 plus 495, which gives us a total of 1089.

[*Now ask the person to hold up the card which you had prepared after reading the children's minds. The congregation will be most impressed!*]

Well, boys and girls, do you think I *really* read your minds? I will have to be honest and say that I did not. What you have seen is really just an old party trick involving numbers.

And yet, although I can't read your minds, there is one who can. God can do that. God knows the thoughts of our minds and the feelings of all our hearts. He knows when we are anxious and afraid. He knows when we are disappointed and lonely. He knows when we are sad. God knows and understands what we are feeling.

That is why the words of the Psalmist make a fitting prayer for all of us, as we begin a new week: '*Search me, O God, and know my heart! Try me, and know my thoughts! And see if there be any wicked way in me, and lead me in the way everlasting!*'

◆ PRAYER –
[*Use the words of the text yet again, the children repeating it, phrase by phrase.*]

Hameldaeme

◆ OCCASION – For the start of Sunday School

◆ TEXT – Psalm 122: 1
'I was glad when they said to me, "Let us go to the house of the Lord!"'

◆ VISUAL AID –
A card with the word 'Hameldaeme' printed on it

BOYS and girls, I hope you all had a good summer holiday. Today we welcome you back to church as the new Sunday School session begins.

A few weeks ago people were asking the question, 'Where are you going for your summer holidays?' So today let me ask you, where did you go for your holidays? [*Allow a few replies and descriptions of the holiday.*]

You know, years ago, when people were asked the question, 'Where are you going for your holidays?', sometimes the reply given was what I have written on this card, 'Hameldaeme'. [*Hold up card.*] Have you ever heard of it? It sounds like a beautiful spot somewhere in the Highlands, but 'Hameldaeme' simply means, 'Home will do me'. In other words, those who gave that reply were not going away on holiday at all. They were going to spend their holiday at home without going away. Their own home would do them.

There is nothing wrong with home, of course, and there is nothing wrong with having a holiday at home either. Home is the place where we are accepted for who we are. Home is the place where we find people who truly love and care for us. In fact, they do that, not because we are always good and pleasant, kind and obedient, but because at home we are still loved, even if we are none of these things. That is why we should always be thankful for our homes and for those who love and care for us there.

If you have ever seen the film 'The Wizard of Oz', then you'll remember how, at the end of the story, the Tin Man asks Dorothy what she has learned from her experience. Dorothy replies, 'If ever I go looking for my heart's desire again, I won't look any further than my own back yard'. Dorothy had learned that the best place in the world is that place where we are surrounded by the love of those who truly care for us – and that place is called HOME.

Today, when we come back to Sunday School, and every time we come to church, I wonder if you realise that you are coming home – home to God's house. Here too there are people who love and care for you, and this is the place where we learn, week by week, of God's love for us all. So, boys and girls, welcome – welcome home!

◆ PRAYER –
Lord God, we thank You for our homes, and for mothers and fathers, brothers and sisters who care for us there. But especially today we thank You for the church where we are always welcome. Grant that today and everyday on which we worship here, we may learn more about You and come to love You more. For Jesus' sake. Amen.

The
Perfect Armour

◆ TEXT – 2 Corinthians 6: 7 (Good News Bible)
'We have righteousness as our weapon.'

◆ VISUAL AID –
A picture of a knight in armour

HOW many of you have seen a knight in armour? I have a picture of one here. [*Show picture.*] Look how the armour protects all the important parts of the knight's body. Even his horse wore a kind of armour to protect from harm. For the knight himself, there was a slit in his helmet so that he could see the enemy, but when all was well, he could lift the visor, as it was called, from his face. It must have been pretty hot in that armour, but I don't suppose the knight minded too much, especially if it saved his life!

What sort of weapons did the knight use? .... Yes, a sword. He also used a lance when he took part in tournaments, or a mace or a wicked-looking ball and chain! They had to be pretty strong in these days, didn't they?

Long, long ago, the Greeks were at war with the Trojans and were camped all around the city of Troy. One of the Greek champions was a man called Achilles. He was a fearsome fellow whom many said could not be killed, because his mother had dipped him, as a baby, in a special river called the River Styx, so that he was like a knight with a suit of invisible armour.

Ah, but even as Achilles rode his chariot round Troy, one of the arrows, shot by the Trojan Paris, hit him in the heel, and he was killed!

64

That, it seems, was his weak spot – because when his mother had bathed him in the river, she had held on to him by the heel, and since the water had not touched him there, his heel was unprotected.

It's strange, but even the best armour has a weakness somewhere, and sooner or later it can be found out. People call that weakness an 'Achilles heel', giving it the name from the story I have just told you.

The only perfect armour is the armour that God provides – truth, faith and love. Paul had one word for that. He called it 'righteousness' or doing what is right. And so he reminded the Corinthians that, as Christian people, *'we have righteousness as our weapon'*.

◆ PRAYER –
Lord, as we live, support us with Your grace, that armed with the weapon of righteousness, we may not be overcome even in our weakest moments. In Jesus' name. Amen.

Welcome

◆ OCCASION – Palm Sunday

◆ VISUAL AID –
A Palm branch, real or false

IN days gone by – not so much nowadays – people used to have a mat at the front door of the house with the word 'Welcome' printed on it. It simply meant what it said. Visitors would be welcome and assured of a warm greeting. Today we still speak about 'putting out the welcome mat' when we are looking forward to someone coming. If you had someone very special coming to visit, you would make sure that everything was just right, so that they knew that you were honouring them.

One day, long ago, some people in Jerusalem were expecting a 'V.I.P.' What does that mean? .... It means a very important person. In this case, the person was Jesus. They had heard of this wonderful teacher, and they wanted to welcome him to the capital city in style. They did something, therefore, which was only done for the most important people. They laid palm branches, rather like this, on the road in front of him, and of course the children enjoyed doing that, more than anyone.

Ever since then, the church has celebrated the Sunday before Easter as Palm Sunday, remembering that day when Jesus rode on a donkey into Jerusalem and into the hearts of some of the people there. So today, on Palm Sunday, we can rejoice, because Jesus still comes seeking a welcome in our hearts.

There is one word of warning though. Many people who cheered Jesus into Jerusalem on that Palm Sunday turned against Him before the week was over. Let's make sure that we never do that. Instead, let's welcome Jesus into our hearts today, and let's ask Him to stay.

◆ PRAYER –

Lord Jesus, as we remember today how You entered the city of Jerusalem where You were to die, and how the people welcomed You with shouts of hosanna and palm branches spread on the road, help us to welcome You into our lives today, so that You may reign there forever. Amen.

The
New Heart

◆ TEXT – Ezekiel 36: 26
  'A new heart I will give you, and a new spirit I will put within you; and I will take out of your flesh the heart of stone and give you a heart of flesh.'

HAVE you ever seen the film, or perhaps read the book, called 'The Wizard of Oz'? .... Good – then let's have a competition this morning between the boys and girls. Try answering these questions, and I will keep the score:

What was the name of the girl in the story?   [*Dorothy*]

Name her dog?   [*Toto*]

Where did the wizard live?   [*The Emerald City*]

What did Scarecrow want?   [*A Brain*]

Where did Dorothy come from?   [*Kansas City*]

[*Ask any other questions you want, if you have time, and keep the score.*]

Well done, both teams, and you really are all winners, for I am sure you *all* knew the answers. There is one question I didn't ask, but I shall ask it now. Here it is. What was it that the Tin Man in the story wanted most of all? .... That's right! He wanted a heart!

68

What a sad situation! What a shame! Such a clever fellow for a man made of tin. He could dance. He could speak. He could sing. He could do so many things. But he had no heart, and to have no heart is to be unable to feel anything.

To have a heart, on the other hand, is a *wonderful* thing – for when we say of anybody that they have a heart, we mean that they can feel love, kindness, pity, sorrow, concern, and all sorts of feelings. And yet to have a heart can also be dangerous, for a heart can carry hatred, anger, spite and bitterness.

That means it is an important thing not only to have a heart, but to have the *right* kind of heart. The prophet Ezekiel in the Old Testament spoke for God to his people, and he said this: '*A new heart will I give you, and a new spirit I will put within you; and I will take out of your flesh the heart of stone, and I will give you a heart of flesh.*'

It is a great thing to have a heart. But it is more important to ask God to give us the right kind of heart – the heart that is not hard and stony, but sensitive to His word and to the needs of other people – a heart of flesh.

◆ PRAYER –
Lord God, give us day by day, the right kind of heart – the heart which truly loves You and which is kind and generous to its neighbour. In Jesus' name. Amen.

The
Two Ways

◆ TEXT – Matthew 7: 13-14
*'Enter by the narrow gate; for the gate is wide and the way is easy, that
leads to destruction, and those who enter by it are many. For the gate is
narrow and the way is hard, that leads to life, and those who find it are
few.'*

SOME time ago, you might remember, we talked about 'The Wizard of
Oz' and all the wonderful characters in the story. We all have our own
favourite, of course, but I liked the Scarecrow! He was so funny, and, in
his own way, he was kind and loving too.

Maybe you remember what happened when Dorothy and the Scarecrow first met?

Dorothy was standing at a crossroads looking puzzled. She said:
'Which way do I go now'?

Just then a voice said, 'Pardon me, but that is a good way'.

Dorothy was startled, and, when she looked around to see who was
speaking, all she could see was a Scarecrow pointing in one direction.

As she turned her back again, the voice spoke again, saying, 'That
way is a good way too', and, turning round again, she noticed that the
Scarecrow was now pointing in the other direction.

Then, as she watched, Scarecrow said, 'Of course, some people do go
both ways'.

Poor Dorothy was annoyed, and she asked, 'Are you doing that on
purpose, or can't you make up your mind?' Scarecrow replied sadly,
'That's the trouble, I can't make up my mind – I haven't got a brain!'

Boys and girls, we do have a brain but we don't always use it! Some-

70

times in life we find ourselves at a crossroads, as it were, with a choice of roads, and we find it difficult to decide which to follow. The trouble is that one way seems hard and rather dull, while the other looks easy and fun! Then we are tempted to choose the easy way, only to discover that it leads to trouble and unhappiness, and we realise too late that the easiest way is not always the right way.

Jesus too reminded his hearers that there are two ways – a broad way which many follow but which only leads to trouble; and a narrow way which few choose but which leads to happiness.

Unlike Scarecrow, whose head, after all, was only filled with straw, Jesus knew that the two ways cannot be good. He told us always to be wary of the broad, easy road that most people rush to take but whose end is disappointment and grief, and to be prepared to take the narrow road which may not be the popular choice and which may appear hard, but, in the end, leads to happiness.

◆ PRAYER –
Lord, teach us that the best way is not always found by following the crowd, and by the guidance of the Holy Spirit direct us in the way that we ought to go. Amen.

The
Watch

◆ TEXT – 2 Corinthians 6: 2
*'Behold, now is the acceptable time;
behold, now is the day of salvation.'*

◆ VISUAL AID –
A wristwatch

BOYS and girls, what has a face and two hands, but no legs? .... Yes, you got that quite easily, didn't you? The answer is a watch.

How many of you have watches? .... Good! And can you tell the time? Ah, but can you tell the time in the 24 hour fashion?

For example, what is 3.00 p.m. on the 24 hour clock? Yes, 15.00 hours. What about 7.30 in the evening? .... Right again, it's 19.30 hours. Here's a really hard one – What is five minutes past midnight? .... Very good! Yes, it would be 00.05 hours. It's not really so difficult to tell the time, is it?

In the old days, people used to tell the time of day by the position of the sun in the sky, or by using a sundial. But that wouldn't be much use to us, when we have so many dull and rainy days. So a watch is a wonderful thing which helps us to keep important appointments. It keeps us in time for school – usually – and it tells us when it is time to gather together for worship.

Let me tell you this, though – there is one time for which you do not need a watch – and that's when it is time to give your love and your service to Jesus. The time for that is always now!

◆ PRAYER –

Lord, help us always to use our time wisely and well. Above all, help us not to delay to offer You the love of our hearts and the service of our lives. Amen.

On Guard

◆ TEXT – Matthew 7: 15-16
'Beware of false prophets, who come to you in sheep's clothing but inwardly are ravenous wolves. You will know them by their fruits.'

BOYS and girls, how many of you know the story of the wooden puppet who wanted to be a real boy? Can you tell me his name? Quite right, he was called Pinnochio. How about a little quiz on the story – boys versus girls? All right, here are the questions:

What was Pinnochio's father called?	*[Gepetto]*
Who was Pinnochio's conscience?	*[Jiminy Cricket]*
Name the cat in the story?	*[Figaro]*
And what was the goldfish called?	*[Cleo]*
What swallowed Pinnochio?	*[A whale]*
What happened if Pinnochio told a lie?	*[His nose grew]*

Well done! So what's the final score? .... Ah well, today it was the turn of the boys [or *girls*] to win!

Just for a moment though, I want to remind you of another character in the story who tricked Pinnochio into going to the carnival instead of school. His name was J. Worthington Longfellow, and he was a wily

74

fox. He lured Pinnochio into terrible danger with his smooth tongue. Anything he promised was lies, but he was very clever at it. Pinnochio was foolish enough to believe him, until he found himself in trouble and saw the result of having listened in the first place.

Jesus spoke about that kind of situation when he gave His warning about false prophets who do their best to lure us into trouble. He said that they might sound very convincing, but told us to judge them by the effect they produced. 'It's a bit like the trees,' he said. 'A healthy tree produces good fruit, while an unhealthy tree produces bad.'

It is a wise lesson to learn, boys and girls, because there are many false prophets around who promise us excitement and happiness, when all the time what they have to offer only leads to sorrow and distress. As Jesus said, we must beware of them, asking whether those who have taken what they offer have really found happiness. There are no short-cuts in life, and there is none to happiness. That only comes by doing what is right, and the way to do that is to follow the way of Jesus who led no one astray, and who only seeks the best for us.

◆ PRAYER –
O God our Father, day by day guide us by Your Spirit, so that we may be defended from those who would harm us and be followers only of that which is good. In Jesus' name. Amen.

The
Neighbour

◆ TEXT – 1 John 4: 21
  '... he who loves God should love his brother also.'

IN a small town, many years ago, there lived a very rich and greedy man. He sold grain to the people so that they could make bread, but he always gave them less than he should have given, and charged them more than he was entitled to charge.

The people were very unhappy about the situation, but did not know what they could do about it. They were particularly unhappy, because the man went to church every Sunday looking very important and sincere. There he would sit in the front seat, always singing the hymns loudly and bending his head low for the prayers. When it was time for the offering, he made a great show of giving his money, although what he gave was not very much at all. Whenever there were church meetings, his was the voice which always rang out to say what should or should not be done. He was, quite simply, a man with two faces – a false one, which he tried to show to God, and a real one which other people saw during the week.

At last, a good soul told the priest what was happening, and he decided to take matters into his own hands. One day, he suddenly appeared when the man was giving out the grain, and, without warning, he took the great serving spoon and began to fill the sacks of the customers until they were bulging. All the while, he smiled at the man saying, 'Do you remember the old chorus, my friend – "Full and running over"?'

The man was furious but he could do nothing, especially as the good

76

old priest reminded him of the verse with which I began, whoever *'loves God should love his brother also'*.

There is no point in ever trying to fool God. If we love Him, then we will also love our neighbours, who are all God's people.

◆ PRAYER –
Lord God, help us now and always to be kind to others, remembering that it is only as we love our neighbour that we show our love for You. In Jesus' name. Amen.

The
Telephone Directory

◆ TEXT – Matthew 10: 31 (Good News Bible)
  ' ... do not be afraid: you are worth much more than sparrows.'

DO you enjoy reading books? .... Yes, I'm sure you do. But do you enjoy reading *all* books? Most of us would have to say that we do not enjoy every book we read. I have some favourite books, but I also have others which are not at all enjoyable to read, although I use them frequently. I have a book like that in this bag this morning. Let's have a look at it.

What is it? ....

Yes, it's a telephone directory.

Now, I would not sit and read this book as I would read a good story. The telephone directory is what we call a reference book. Just like another reference book which most of us use – the dictionary – which contains a long list of words and meanings, the telephone directory contains a list of names and addresses in alphabetical order, and a telephone number beside each.

Yet this, in fact, is probably the most used book in my study, because I consult it frequently to find the telephone numbers of people I want to call.

Just as the dictionary has many words, so the telephone directory has thousands of names, addresses and telephone numbers in it. Indeed, it contains so many names and addresses that it would take me a long time to go through them all, even if I wanted to. I don't do that because most of them are of no importance to me. But there are some which are *very* important to me, so that if they were not to be found here, I would have to spend a great deal of time contacting telephone enquiries to get the numbers.

The reason why the telephone directory is so large and contains so many numbers is that every entry in it is important to someone, especially if you are the someone concerned. Nobody enjoys being left out of something special when their name should be included. For that reason, great care is taken to ensure that no name is missed out. But every entry is important to British Telecom too, because they want their customers to feel that they matter to the company, and that they will regularly use the telephone.

You are important to God, and He knows your name. He doesn't have a directory like British Telecom's, but He keeps all the names of those whom He loves in His heart. You are special and you matter to Him! Jesus once told of how not one sparrow is forgotten by God, and he went on to say, ' ... *do not be afraid: you are worth much more than sparrows'*.

It is quite nice to see our names in the telephone directory, but it is much better to know that we matter to God and that He cares for us.

◆ PRAYER –
Gracious God, we are Yours. You know us by name. You care for us. Help us day by day to live more worthily of Your love. In Jesus' name. Amen.

Radiate!

◆ TEXT – John 13: 34 (Good News Bible)
  'As I have loved you, so you must love one another.'

◆ VISUAL AID –
  A radiator, and a light (or appropriate variables)

TODAY, boys and girls, I haven't brought along the objects for my talk, because they are already here in church. Just look over to the wall there, and to that cast iron thing with ribs running up and down. What do we call that object? .... That's it – a radiator! You may have a radiator at home which looks different to this. Indeed, in some churches and halls there are radiant heaters which are placed high on the wall and which glow when they are switched on.

The words 'radiator' and 'radiant' are quite alike. Both come from the word 'radiate'. That is a difficult word to understand, so I went to the dictionary to find its meaning. There I read, 'Radiate: emit rays of light or heat'. Now, since 'emit' simply means 'send out', *to radiate* is *to send out rays*. Radiators and radiant heaters send out rays of heat.

But the dictionary also speaks about sending out light rays. That means that candles and light bulbs and torches *radiate*. They emit or send out light.

[*At this point, one could switch on an overhead projector or a powerful torch to demonstrate light rays.*]

Now, boys and girls, I want you to join me in saying something important. Repeat after me, 'I am a radiator' ....

Does that seem a strange thing to say? Let me explain what I mean.

One day, Jesus was giving the people what He called 'a new commandment', and He finished with the words, *'As I have loved you, so you must love one another'*.

Do you believe that Jesus loves you? Yes, of course you do: so you will love others as He has loved you. That is what makes you a 'radiator'. You send out the love of Jesus, the love that you have received from Him, in loving other people.

So once again will you repeat the words after me, 'I am a radiator'.

Wonderful! We are going to radiate the love of Jesus wherever we go. Heater radiators will send out heat. Light radiators will send out light. And love radiators will send out the love that Jesus has shown to them.

◆ PRAYER –
Lord God, help us so to live, that we may spread the love of Jesus wherever we are and among all whom we meet. In Jesus' name. Amen.

Unchanging

◆ TEXT – Hebrews 13: 8
'*Jesus Christ is the same yesterday and today and forever.'*

◆ VISUAL AID –
Some black and white photographs of bygone days

TODAY I have in my hand some things that go back a long time. [*Hold up photographs.*] These are photographs taken many years ago, long before any of you were born. When you look at them, you notice that some things in them are just the same as they are today, but some things are quite different.

Tell me, what things do you notice that are different from today? .... Well the clothes are different in fashion, the cars are different in shape, and the haircuts are different in style. Even the toys children have are different. There is no sign of electronic games or battery-operated toys in any of these pictures.

What do you think has *not* changed? Let me help you with the answer I am looking for. *People* have not changed! Oh I know, in one sense the *individuals* in these photographs have changed, for some, in the very old ones, have died, while those in the others have clearly grown older. But I am not talking about people as individuals, but people in general. What I mean is that people still go about the business of life, just as they always did, doing the same kinds of things. They play games. They go on picnics. They fall in love and marry. The outer things may alter – like clothes and cars and hairstyles and toys – but people remain much the same in what they do, and in the way they think and feel.

We can certainly see that these photographs are not up-to-date. They were taken when colour photography was still uncommon – almost everyone today takes colour photographs. Sometimes my family have great fun with the old black and white photos which I have kept from boyhood. They bring them out when their friends visit, and then they roll about with laughter at how strange life must have been when Dad was a boy – compared to today.

With most things in our world we have to get up-to-date, but at the same time we have to remember that some things *don't* change. It's like that with our Christian faith. Much about it has to get up-to-date, like the way we worship, the songs and hymns we sing and the kind of churches we build. But the person at the centre of our faith never changes. That is why the writer tells us that *'Jesus Christ is the same yesterday and today and forever'.*

It is good to know that, because while our styles and surroundings change, the One in whom we put our trust never changes. I would encourage each of you now to put your faith in Jesus. Then, no matter how the years pass on, you will have a friend and companion who will always be the same.

◆ PRAYER –
Lord God, we thank You for the promise of Jesus that He is with us always even to the end of the age, and we thank You that He is still the same, our guide, our hero and our friend. Hear our thanksgiving in His name. Amen.

Seeing clearly

◆ TEXT – Mark 8: 25
' ... he laid his hand upon his eyes; and he looked intently and was restored, and saw everything clearly.'

◆ VISUAL AID –
A pair of ordinary spectacles, and a pair of sun-glasses

BOYS and girls, I have with me a pair of ordinary glasses (which can also be called spectacles), and a pair of sun-glasses.

Let me try on the sun-glasses first. These are not very helpful inside the building here, because when I wear them I can't see very well. The sun-glasses make it difficult for me to see some of the things around me. As I look through them it is too dark to see clearly inside the church building.

Now let me try on these ordinary glasses. Yes! That's much better. Not only can I see very clearly through them, but, because they magnify slightly what is around me, I can see things in much greater detail. In fact, the small print in this hymnbook which I can hardly see with my bare eyes, and which I cannot see at all through sun-glasses, is now as clear as can be whenever I look at it through my spectacles!

But things can be very different when I go out into the sunlight. There, with ordinary spectacles on, my eyes can be dazzled by the brightness of the light, whereas the sun-glasses give me some shade and allow me to open my eyes and see what is in front of me much more comfortably.

The truth of the matter is that there are right times for each pair of glasses. Use them wrongly and they don't help at all. I could never find a pin in a room while wearing sun-glasses, but with my spectacles on I would find it very quickly. On the other hand, I would find it difficult to read a page of a book in bright, direct sunlight while wearing ordinary spectacles, but, when I reduce the brightness of the light by wearing what are now known as 'shades', I can see the words on the page quite clearly.

There is a lovely story in Mark's gospel which tells of Jesus meeting a blind man. Jesus put his hands on his eyes and asked him if he could see anything.

'I can see people,' he replied, 'but they look like trees walking about.'

So Jesus put his hands on the man's eyes a second time, and the Bible says that this time the man saw everything clearly.

Jesus did not want the man to have second best. He wanted him to have the best vision possible. Indeed, just as He helped the blind man, so Jesus can help us to see clearly, not so much what is in front of our eyes, but what is His will for us.

Sometimes Christian people find it difficult to know what Jesus requires of them, and when that happens they pray to Him and ask Him to help them see what He wants them to do for Him. Or sometimes they have problems understanding the Bible, and ask Him in prayer to guide them to a clear understanding of it.

Why don't you ask Jesus in your prayers to help you 'see' more clearly what His word says, and what His will is for you?

◆ PRAYER –
Lord God, today and everyday, help us to see You are with us to support and to guide, and help us also to see what You want us to do and be. For Jesus' sake. Amen.

Comfortable Fitting

◆ TEXT – Matthew 11: 30
  'For my yoke is easy, and my burden is light.'

◆ VISUAL AID –
  A pair of shoes

BOYS and girls, what has eyes, a tongue, a toe, a heel and a sole? That's right – a pair of shoes. Here is a pair of my shoes, and I can point to all the parts I have have mentioned – eyes, tongue, toe, heel and sole.

Most of us have different kinds of shoes which we wear on different occasions. So, for example, we might have shoes for daily wear, and shoes for walking and climbing on rough ground. Then, in addition to these, we might also have trainers and dress shoes.

Some people find a pair of shoes so comfortable that they wear them until they are almost falling off their feet, and some people have shoes that make them feel really happy. When I was a boy there was a song which had the line, 'shoes to set my feet a-dancing'. These must have been very happy shoes indeed!

I'm sure you have a favourite pair of shoes. Perhaps you wear them so often that, when you put them on, your parents say to you, 'Not *that* pair of shoes again'! And you say in return, 'But *they're* so comfortable'!

Many years ago in China, ladies used to have their feet bound with bandages to prevent them from growing larger. There, if a woman had tiny feet, it was considered a thing of beauty. However, because they had had their feet bound when they were young, many of the women had to suffer great pain throughout their lives. The very thought of it makes me feel sore. I like my feet to be in comfortable fitting shoes and the idea of forcing them into something smaller doesn't bear thinking about.

Jesus once told the people that His way would fit them very comfortably. He was talking to people who believed that, if they were to find favour with God, they would have to earn it by keeping hundreds of rules that affected everything they did every day. No wonder they found it hard and uncomfortable and even felt sore with the strain.

Jesus said to these people that His way would fit them as comfortably as a yoke was meant to fit the oxen ploughing a field. *'Come to me, all ye who labour and are heavy laden, and I will give you rest,'* He told them. *'Take my yoke upon you, and learn from me; for I am gentle and lowly in heart, and you will find rest for your souls. For my yoke is easy, and my burden is light.'*

Today, of course, we don't see oxen pulling ploughs over fields, and it may be that if Jesus were speaking today, He would say that His way fitted, not like a yoke for an ox, but just like a comfortable pair of shoes.

To follow His way means that we will love God and our fellows, and while that may not always be the easiest thing to do, when we remember the love of God for us, then the duty which is asked of us becomes a joy.

I was going to say, in closing, that there is nothing better than to fit into a pair of very comfortable shoes, but there is. It is to fit into the way that Jesus has shown us.

◆ PRAYER –
Lord, as we live, help us to follow the way of Jesus, the way of love to You and to others, and so live the kind of life for which we were made. In Jesus' name. Amen.

Bath
Pearls

◆ TEXT – 2 Corinthians 2: 15
'For we are the aroma of Christ ... '

◆ VISUAL AID –
A small bottle of bath pearls

THIS morning I have brought a collection of these little spheres.

I wonder if anyone knows what they are? Marbles .... No! Sweets .... No! In fact, you would soon have a very nasty taste in your mouth, if you tried to eat one of these.

I'll tell you what they are. They are bath pearls. You take one or two, drop them in the warm water of your bath, and, in a short time, a lovely smell rises from the water. Then, if you put your hands in and gently splash the bath water about, you get lots and lots of bubbles. Do you like bubbles in your bath? ....

When I was a boy, I sometimes made a beard with the bubbles, but they soon disappeared and I was left with a soapy film on my face. Sometimes I was left with a soapy taste in my mouth too, but that is something you learn from experience.

Locked away inside these little pearls is some soapy liquid with a nice perfume in it. Indeed, you can buy different kinds of pearls and these produce a variety of nice smells. What happens when we put them in our bath? As if by magic, the outer coating of the 'pearl' just melts away, and all the loveliness of the perfume flows out into the water.

Think of the whole wide world like a bath full of water, and think of yourself as one little bath pearl. You would like to bring loveliness and goodness into the world wouldn't you?

Sadly, not all people do that. Some bring unkindness and cruelty into the world. That is like having bath pearls with nasty smelling liquid instead of perfume, and grit instead of soap. You would soon get rid of these from your bath because they would make you feel very uncomfortable.

St Paul once said, in a letter to the church at Corinth, *'we are the aroma of Christ'*. He was saying that, wherever we go, we should, as Christian people, be like the melting bath pearl creating a lovely fragrance. To everyone we meet, we should spread the goodness and the care for others that Jesus did, and so make the world a lovelier place.

◆ PRAYER –

Lord God, by our words and deeds, help us to bring to the world the goodness, the kindness, the truth and the joy that Jesus brought. In His name. Amen.

Fruit
Salad

◆ TEXT – 1 Thessalonians 5: 9-10 (adapted from Good News Bible)
'God did not choose us to suffer his wrath, but to possess salvation through our Lord Jesus Christ, who died for us in order that we might live together with him.'

◆ VISUAL AID –
A variety of different fruits

TODAY, boys and girls, my mouth is watering even before I begin. The reason is that I have brought to church a number of different fruits. There is an apple, an orange, a plum, some grapes, and I mustn't forget my own favourite, a banana. I'm sure that, out of these, you too have a favourite. I wonder what it is? Let's have a vote on it this morning. Hands up if the fruit I hold is your favourite. [*Proceed to display the different fruits.*]

All of these are good in their own ways. One is harder than the others [*apple*]. One is juicier [*orange*]. One has a large stone [*plum*]. One seems to have no stones at all [*banana*]. One is shaped like a light bulb [*pear*]. One is smaller than all the others, so that we need a few of them [*grape*]. They all look different on the outside, but, when it comes to the inside they all have one thing in common. They are good to taste.

One other thing comes to mind. Although each of these fruits can taste very good on their own, I like them best when they are prepared and put together to make up a fruit salad. It is probably my favourite kind of pudding course.

Let's just think about people in the same way. I mean, just like the

90

fruits, we all look quite different on the outside. We have different features – different colours of hair or even no hair at all, different shades of skin, different heights and different sizes of tummies! Yet inside each of us there is something that is the same. Each of us has a heart, and our heart stirs us to do good.

Perhaps, like fruit, there are some people that we like better than others, but that does not take away from each one being important to God. How generous He was when he created all the people and all the fruits because he made both in such varieties!

But there is something else I want to say about the differences between people – for, just like the fruit salad, when the people who love Jesus are united they are wonderful! St Paul had that in mind when he wrote the words of our text to the church at Thessalonica: *'God did not choose us to suffer his wrath, but to possess salvation through our Lord Jesus Christ, who died for us in order that we might live together with Him.'*

That tells us Jesus died for us in order to take away our sins, so that, if we become His followers, we will live together in harmony and peace with one another. We don't want to be enemies with others. We want to be friends with everyone. And that will make the kind of world God planned when he put into it different fruits and different people because he delighted in such varieties.

Although in this church today we are all different on the outside, let us remain the same in faith and love for Jesus on the inside.

◆ PRAYER –
Father God, we thank You for the richness and the variety of people in Your world. Help us to live in peace and harmony with them all, and in Your church bind us together as one to Your glory. In Jesus' name. Amen.

The
Onion

◆ TEXT – John 1: 29
  'Behold, the Lamb of God, who takes away the sin of the world!'

◆ VISUAL AID –
  An onion

I WONDER who can tell me what *this* is? [*Hold up onion.*] Yes, that's right. It's an onion. If you're like me, then you will like onions. I enjoy eating them raw in salads, and I like them cooked in soups, stews and sauces. They are among the most useful of vegetables because they provide lots of flavour. Yet, for all its good qualities, the onion has a number of drawbacks.

To begin with, when you peel an onion your eyes begin to water. Some people suggest that putting a teaspoon in your mouth, while you peel or cut, prevents this from happening. I have tried it, and I think it works, but only a little bit! Most times I still end up crying as if I were watching a very sad film!

Or again, after you have finished cutting and peeling an onion, its smell lingers on your hands, and, no matter how you try to wash it away, it just seems to come back again and again before eventually wearing off.

But not only does the onion leave a smell on our hands. It does the same everywhere else. In a kitchen where onions have been fried, the smell remains for hours. And, of course, although we don't like to talk about it, the onion leaves a smell on our breath for a long time too.

Some other things in life are a bit like the onion, in that their effect lasts for a long time. Sins are like that. Temptations come, and we give in to them, and they leave their effect on us. We do something unkind to a friend, and that friendship is broken for some time to come. We say something nasty about a classmate, and it remains with them for many days.

Eventually we can be rid of the smells of the onion. It takes time, together with much scrubbing of the hands and spraying the air with aerosols. There are even theories about how to make our breath smell better.

Unfortunately, getting rid of our sins is not as simple as that. And yet, although their effects stay with us for a long time, there is a way to be rid of our sins quickly and for all time. John the Baptist once said of Jesus, *'Behold, the Lamb of God, who takes away the sin of the world!'* Since such an amazing claim was made of Jesus, it will be no problem for Him to take away your sins and mine. Let's ask Him to do that. Let's ask Him to come into our life and remove our sin now and forever.

◆ PRAYER –
Father, we thank You for Jesus who came to save us from our sins. Help us now and everyday to live the new life which He offers us. For Your love's sake, Amen.

Power

◆ TEXT – Acts 1: 8 (adapted from RSV)
'... you shall receive power when the Holy Spirit has come upon you; and you shall be my witnesses ...'

◆ VISUAL AID –
A battery charger and some batteries.

LAST night, boys and girls, I met a 'Good Samaritan'. That is the name of a bible character who went to the help of another man in need.

Last night I needed to use my torch and I discovered that my batteries had run out. The friend, whom I was visiting, said that he had some batteries, but they turned out to be as dead as my own. Then he said that if I waited about an hour, he could put enough power into them to light up my torch bulb. So the batteries were placed in a battery charger, and, in a short time, my torch was working again.

That reminded me of a time when a much larger battery failed me. On that occasion it was my car battery. Since I was far away from a battery charger, the car needed to be push started, but I was the only person there. Eventually a Good Samaritan came along and tried to push, but that was not enough. Two more came and added their weight, but, no matter how hard they tried, they could not get enough speed up for the car to kick start.

Then, at last, another man came on the scene. 'I have a rope in my car,' he shouted, 'I'll give you a tow, and we'll see if it starts that way.'

So he positioned his car in front of mine, brought out a rope from his boot, and tied one end under the back of his car and the other to a firm bit of metal under the front of mine. Then, as he drove off, I slipped my car into gear and lifted the clutch, and a few hundred yards on my engine coughed and spluttered into life and began to run quite nicely, allowing the dynamo to take over and recharge the battery.

In both incidents, what I needed was power – power to get the batteries charged. In the case of the car, I needed a great deal of power to get going. Three people pushing were not enough. It took the engine of the other car to give me the power necessary.

There is another kind of power that we need in life. It is the power to do what is right, to love what is good and gracious, and to be the kind of people God wants us to be. Perhaps you have tried to be like that, but have failed. You found that temptation came along and weakened you, and you gave in.

That is when we need the power that comes from Jesus. He told His disciples, 'You shall receive power when the Holy Spirit has come upon you; and you shall be my witnesses'. I think we should all ask Jesus to give us the power of the Holy Spirit, to be strong against evil, and to be bold in showing others that we are His followers.

◆ PRAYER –
Lord God, by Your Holy Spirit, give us the power to live as You would have us live. In Jesus' name. Amen.

Part 2

The
FAMILY SERVICE

by

Iain Roy

The
Family Service

◆ INTRODUCTION

IF ministers find Children's Addresses difficult, they often find Family Services impossible. The nub of the problem lies in the age range of those worshipping.

Take heart. The task is not impossible. But it does need application and effort to overcome. A Family Service will usually take much more time to prepare than an ordinary act of worship.

It requires the use of gifts, not just the minister's but those of the children and adults in the congregation. It also requires a recognition of limitations, both one's own and those of other people. A cardinal rule for the minister in particular is – if you cannot do something yourself, get someone else who can. It may even mean, for some ministers with limited gifts in this area, getting someone else to take the major part of the service. But always make sure that you have at least a part in it, to show that you are behind this kind of worship, and always support each individual and group participating. DON'T JUST LEAVE THEM TO GET ON WITH IT!

The congregation, though one on the Sunday of a Family service, worshipping as they are in one place, must be recognised as having different constituent parts, each of which has its own needs and level of participation.

There is the **Pre-School Group**, and the aim with them must be to keep their interest by the liveliness of the activity of worship. They like things to be happening. For them, words alone are not enough. They need the impact of the visual. They can respond to humour, and are interested in what older youngsters are doing. They are happy to 'come out to the front' and use simple skills – stick a picture on, feel something, taste something, hold something. DO NOT UNDERESTIMATE THEM! They can show knowledge which will surprise you, and give answers to questions that you would never expect. Our basic aim must be to make them feel secure and happy in Church, to enable them to feel wanted there, and to help them feel that Church is a place where they want to be.

The **Sunday School/Bible Class** are the power-house of the Family Service. They participate fully in it by their questions and answers, their preparation of prayer, praise, drama, frieze or handwork. They sometimes prepare for the worship by a special project leading up to it, or sometimes a special project has the Family Service as its starting point.

Above all, it is through them and their response that the ADULTS themselves must be stimulated in the worship either to learn with the youngsters, or to see, through the youngsters' participation, how they themselves should worship and celebrate. Much is made of the need for adults to give a lead to children. Jesus, however, made the point that children can lead adults (Matthew 18: 2-4). Perhaps this is an idea that we should take more seriously. The freshness, spontaneity, enthusiasm and commitment of youngsters can help revive even the most jaded adults.

The services which follow are not meant to be 'off-the-peg' services for use in Family Worship, so much as illustration and encouragement to create your own. Rarely can worship suitable for one congregation perfectly fit another. Yet, all of us can benefit from others' ideas, and adaptation of what others have created is in itself an original skill, as television alone can show.

There will, of course, always be some, in any congregation, who will absent themselves from Family Services on the basis that they cannot stand the noise, or live with the activity. We have to accept that this may not always be just 'grumpiness' on their part. Sometimes it can be the result of poor hearing, or even a nervous edginess. That does not mean that we should abandon this approach, only that we should ration it throughout the whole worshipping year, so that we do try to cater for all the varied needs of our congregation, the whole people of God, young and old.

I normally restrict Family Services to specific occasions:

1 The opening and closing of the Sunday School which is celebrated as an event in our public worship, and not, as so often, a non-event or an ignored event taking place unseen in the Church halls;

2 Harvest Thanksgiving;

3 The Children's Christmas Gift service when the children bring gifts for children in need;

4 The first and last Sundays of the year when our Sunday School teachers have a well-deserved rest;

5 Palm Sunday, when our daily Holy Week services start with a Family Service;

6 Occasionally, however, a Family Service might result from a special Sunday School project, or, as in one case below, mark the beginning of such a project.

Sometimes, of course, it may be difficult to sustain a whole service by an all-ages approach. Perhaps the subject matter does not lend itself to such extended treatment for a whole service, or perhaps our inspiration grows dim. Then we should not hesitate to make it 'partial'.

It is perfectly possible, for instance, in a Harvest Service to have a substantial part of it as a Family Service and then allow the youngsters to go to Sunday School to have something more specific to themselves, while the minister preaches an adult sermon on an appropriate theme. It may even be that the youngsters and teachers can have the harvest gifts ready for immediate distribution at the close of worship.

A Christmas service can have a similar approach, and even the open-

100

ing service of the Sunday School when the children can go from Church after a substantial family act of worship, and the remainder of the time be spent on the simple administration necessary at the beginning of a session.

Flexibility is essential – flexibility of approach, attitude, liturgy and activity. Linked to this must be the creative use of imagination. In an age when the Church is struggling to keep hold of, or attract young people, we have to use every possible means to confront them with the challenge of faith. The Family Service is just one weapon in our armoury.

Iain Roy 1997

An Opening Act of Worship for a Sunday School Year

◆ OPENING HYMN – [*during which the children and their teachers process into the church, pews having been carefully left for them at the front. The act of procession heightens the importance of the occasion and their being there.*]

◆ PRAYER – [*often a rhyming prayer, but always, as here, a simple prayer, a phrase at a time spoken by the minister and then repeated by the whole congregation.*]

> Here we are, O God, to meet You.
> In Your House, dear Lord, to seek You.
> Praise and prayer, O Lord, to give You.
> Truth and love, O Christ, to live for.
> Young and old, Jesus, to trust You.
> Each one seeking, Lord, to serve You.

◆ A CHILDREN'S HYMN –

FIRST SECTION

[*The minister, at lectern to the side of the communion table, scratches his head.*]

Minister: You know, I'm sure I've forgotten something or someone! Are you *all* here? Put up your hand if you're not!

[*A probationer (it could be one of the Sunday School teachers, a Session Clerk, etc) rushes in quite breathless, carrying a suitcase. He/She takes up position on the other side of the communion table.*]

Fiona: Mr Roy! Mr Roy! Did you forget me? Didn't you remember I was here?

Minister: [*Turning to children*] See, I told you. I *knew* I had forgotten somebody or something. Oh, this is terrible. Fancy forgetting Fiona. [*In a whispered aside.*] She'll go in the huff. But really it *is* terrible to have forgotten her or indeed anyone else. One of the things we must always try to make sure of in Church is that EVERYBODY is here. If even ONE person is missing, our Church family is incomplete. Still [*with a sigh of relief*] everybody is here NOW.

Fiona: [*Coughs politely*] Mr Roy … what about – Jimmy?

Minister: [*Puzzled*] Jimmy? [*Light dawns*] Oh, *Jimmy!* Where is he?

Fiona: In here [*pointing to suitcase*].

Minister: In *there!* What is he doing in there? He'll be suffocated! Really, Fiona, don't you think that's a bit careless?

Fiona: Well, he needs assembled.

Minister: [*Horrified*] You mean he is in there – in *bits*?

Fiona: [*Nervously*] Mm-uhuh!

Minister: *Fiona!* Well, we better do something about that. Will you help us, girls and boys, to get Jimmy together?

But first we need a blackboard [*put it in position*]. Right, Fiona, see if you can put Jimmy together now with the help of the boys and girls.

Fiona: [*Taking out the bits and pieces of Jimmy, a cardboard cut-out figure, Fiona asks the children about the different parts of his body in a kind of repartee: she holds her nose when the feet come out, and gets an eye to wink. As a hand and arm come out, she lets it get out of control, slapping and tickling her until she slaps it and gets it under control ... the children locate the parts until Jimmy starts to appear on the board. But still one or two parts of him are missing.*]

Well, that's him, Mr Roy – Jimmy's all here.

Minister: Well, Fiona, he may be *here,* but he's not all *there!* If you ask me, there are still some bits missing. What do you think, girls and boys? You better look again in your case!

Fiona: [*Looking up with horrified expression on her face*] Mr Roy ...

Minister: Yes, Fiona?

Fiona: They're missing!

Minister: *Missing!?* Well, you better find them. Some of the boys and girls will go with you. Maybe you've left them in the vestry, or the kitchen, or the hall. [*A search party goes and finds the missing parts, and, on return, puts them in position on the blackboard.*]

Minister: Right. That's Jimmy here now. Would you like to know his full name? Tell them, Fiona.

Fiona: Jimmy Hay.

Minister: No, no, Fiona, how many times do I have to tell you? Not Jimmy Hay … *Hey, Jimmy!*

Now, there is a wee song I would like to teach you. It is about the bits of our body and how they are all connected to each other.

◆ HYMN –
'Head and Shoulders, Knees and Toes' –
no. 46, *Abracadabra Guitar* [A & C Black]

◆ OFFERING AND OFFERING PRAYER –

SECOND SECTION

Minister: Fiona [*or one of the children*] is going to read something from the Bible.

◆ READING –
I Corinthians 12: 12-20

Minister: The Church is a body – Christ's body, to do his work in the world.

Fiona: Yes, Mr Roy – and just like Jimmy every bit of that body is necessary and needs to be in good working order. So we have our eyes and our ears to see and to listen, especially to see the needs of others and to hear their cries for help. We have our feet and hands so that we can go to the help of others. We have our lips so that we can talk to each other, laugh with each other, praise and sing. Let us use our voices now to sing God's praise.

◆ HYMN –
'He Gave Me Eyes' –
no. 19, *Someone's Singing, Lord* [A & C Black]

THIRD SECTION

Fiona: I don't think Mr Roy is looking too well. What do you
           think, boys and girls? You know, I'm not sure if he's fit. I
           don't think Jimmy looks too fit either. [*Looks at children
           and whispers to minister*] Don't you think they look a right
           bunch of couch potatoes?

Minister: Well, we will have to do something about that. [*Gets the
           children to do some simple exercises.*] In church we all have to
           be fit. We are the Body of Christ and each of us has to be fit
           to play our part in Christ's work – the organist, the choir,
           the Sunday School teachers, the elders, *etc.* AND YOU!
           That is why we come to church – to make ourselves fit for
           Christ's service.

Fiona: That is why we read the Bible. That is why we pray to
           God. That is why we sing his praise. It is to make us fit to
           be Christ's body, his Church in the world. And everyone of
           us has something to bring to his work, just as every limb
           in our body has its own part to play. Let us sing a hymn
           that asks us to bring our own specific gifts to Christ's
           service.

◆ HYMN –
'The Wise may bring their Learning' –
no. 464, *Church Hymnary Third Edition* (CH3)
[Oxford University Press]

FOURTH SECTION

Minister: Well, I'm glad we are all here today and learning to work together.

Fiona: [*Coughs to interrupt.*] Mr Roy, Mr Roy, you've forgotten somebody.

Minister: Have I?

Fiona: Yes, our newest recruit.

Minister: Oh, thanks, Fiona. I nearly forgot. Well, we better have the baby in. Let us sing our baptismal hymn.

◆ BAPTISM –

◆ CLOSING HYMN AND BENEDICTION –

A Harvest Thanksgiving

◆ OPENING HYMN – [*Children enter Church.*]

◆ PRAYER –

Minister: [*Asks some questions:*]

How many months are there in a year?   [*twelve*]
How many seasons?   [*four*]
What are the four?   [*Spring, Summer, Autumn, Winter*]

[*Minister holds up some pictures of different seasons.*]

What season would this picture be about? And this?

[*Every primary school has pictures which can be borrowed for this purpose. As each correct answer is given, the child answering comes out and holds the appropriate picture. The pictures have not been shown in seasonal order, but the minister now gets the children to put them in order, moving those holding the pictures about on the instructions of the youngsters.*]

Have we got them in the right order now?

Which season are we in now?

Here is a frieze which the Sunday School has prepared for Autumn.

[This has been part of a project leading up to the service. The minister highlights some features of it which depict Autumn.]

The Sunday School is now going to sing a hymn learned for today.

◆ HYMN – 'Autumn Days' –
no. 4, *Come and Praise* (Book 1) [BBC Books]

[Later the congregation learn it and join in.]

◆ READING – Genesis 8: 20-22

◆ HYMN – 'Fill your Hearts with Song and Gladness' –
no. 9, *Come and Praise* Book 1 [BBC Books]

SECOND SECTION

Minister: Autumn is the time for harvest, especially the harvest of the corn. But all year round, in other lands, different harvests are gathered in. Just as well, or we would not have enough to eat! Now, all your gifts are lying here on our communion table. But there are two other tables specially laid with harvest gifts. I wonder if you notice anything about these two tables, a difference between them? Yes, one is set with food we grow ourselves. The other is set with food that is grown in other countries of the world.

[Item by item, the minister lifts up the food on this table and the children help him to identify the countries where the food is grown.]

You see how much we depend on other countries for our harvest. Let us thank God now for these places, this food, and the people who grow it for us.

109

◆ PRAYER –

> *We thank you, Lord, for all we eat,*
> *For the farmer's field, and the ocean deep,*
> *For those who work the whole year round*
> *Taking the harvest from the ground.*
>
> *We pray now, Lord, for all who live*
> *In distant lands where life is hard.*
> *Give them shelter, clothes and food.*
> *May they know, too, that life is good.*

THIRD SECTION

Minister: Lots of the food we like to eat are mentioned in the Bible. I have asked some people to read now from different parts of the Bible. Listen carefully, and see if you can spot all the different fruits in the Bible passages.

◆ A POT-POURRI OF BIBLE READINGS –
2 Samuel 16: 1-2; Song of Solomon 2: 3; Song of Solomon 2: 11-13a;
Luke 6: 43-45

Minister: Wonderful, isn't it? All the different fruits that are mentioned in the Bible! They LOOK different – in shape, in size, in colour. They TASTE different. Perhaps you would like to play a tasting game with me now?

[*The volunteers are blindfolded.*
Fruits like grapes, bananas, apples can be used.]

◆ HYMN –
'Pears and Apples, Wheat and Grapes' –
no. 135, *Come and Praise* (Book 2) [BBC Books]

110

[The hymn can have been learned by the youngsters beforehand, or taught to them by someone who uses some of the objects on the harvest table to teach folk the first verse. In this way the whole congregation can learn to sing a verse without a single hymn-sheet in sight!]

FOURTH SECTION

Minister: The Jews had several harvest festivals. There was the Passover, the Corn Harvest Festival, and the Festival of Shelters with its summer fruits.

At each harvest festival they gave thanks and always in the same way – by bringing a special gift to the altar. Because they were glad to receive, they were equally glad to give. That is still the reason why we bring our harvest gifts today – glad to receive, we are glad to give.

And, as we give, we give thanks to God for ALL the seasons, and the gifts from EVERY harvest. WE give thanks for ALL who grow our food, and for the variety of food we have to eat. We bring our harvest gifts, as we bring our offerings every week, to give them to God, asking him to use them to bless others as He has blessed us.

◆ THE OFFERING –

◆ A PRAYER –

> *Lord, bless our gifts.*
> *Use them to care*
> *For people here*
> *And everywhere.*

◆ CLOSING HYMN –

◆ BENEDICTION –

A
Christmas Service

[*The children of the Sunday School prepared the praise over a number of weeks, and children and adults acted as broadcasters from around the world.*]

[*There is a table centre with what appears to be broadcasting equipment on it, The producer speaks to the congregation. He is wearing earphones.*]

Producer: Hello, folks. I'm very glad you've all arrived in time for our service. It won't be long now till we go live to our partners around the world in our Christmas broadcast, I wonder if we could just try to establish voice levels. Mr Roy, would you care to start? [*The minister sounds a little nervous as he complies.*] Good, good – I think that will do. Now, I wonder if we could just have a verse of 'Child in the manger'. Gillian [*to the organist*] – are you ready?

Organist: Do you want a little intro?

Producer: Yes, definitely a little intro. Mr Roy, will you bring the congregation in on the verse? Intro, then Gillian, after the countdown – 5 … 4 … 3 … 2 … 1.

[*The Intro is played, then the congregation sing first verse.*]

Good, good … Men, maybe a little more tenor and bass, please.

[*Telephone rings. He answers it.*] Yes, yes, yes.
[*Puts telephone down.*] Two minutes, folks! Silence now!

[*Puts finger to mouth in indication, looks intently at watch. Observes two minutes silence, but as last ten seconds come, he mouths silently to congregation: 10 ... 9 ... 8 ... 7 ... 6 ... 5 ... 4 ... 3 ... 2 ... 1. He indi*cates red light glowing on table. *Points to minister.*]

Minister: Good morning, Boglemart Sound [*a local street name*] welcomes listeners to its shortwave transmission for the Sunday prior to Christmas. Today we are joined by listeners and worshippers in France, Austria and the Czech Republic in the Continent of Europe, from Barbados in the West Indies, and Nicaragua in South America. Let's see if they are receiving us loud and clear. Good morning Aubagne in Provence in France and a Merry Christmas to you.

France: Bonjour, Ecosse – Joyeux Noel.

[*The reply could be broadcast on sound equipment into the sanctuary, or, as in our case, you could set up tables in various areas visible to the congregation from which the answers come.*]

Minister: Good morning, Innsbruck.

Austria: Ach, Guten Morgen, Boglemart Sound in Schottland. Fröhliche Weihnachten.

Minister: Good morning, Prague, and a Merry Christmas to you.

Prague: Versek Vannoch, Boglemart.

Minister: Bueunos dies, Nicaragua.

113

Nicaragua: Good day to you and Merry Christmas, Scotland.

Minister: Ah, your English is ever so much better than my Spanish, Nicaragua.

West Indies: We'll save you the embarrassment of trying out your West Indian. Good morning and Merry Christmas, Boglemart Sound.

Minister: Well, now that we have established that everyone is in hearing distance, I hope that we are going to have a really happy service. Each country is going to contribute one of its very own Christmas carols and tell us something about their Christmas customs. In this way we will widen our celebration into a great big family occasion around the world, all of us celebrating the birth of Jesus. So, first, we go to Provence in France, to the town of Aubagne. I believe your town is very famous for its crèches? Can you explain to us what a crèche is, Aubagne?

France: Oui. A crèche is what you in Scotland would call a Christmas Nativity Scene with little figures. St Francis of Assissi is said to have introduced this idea. Here in Aubagne we have been making little nativity figures of unbaked clay for hundreds of years and exporting them to different parts of the world.

Minister: That is very interesting, Aubagne. Now I believe that you have a fellow called Père Noel who delivers presents to the girls and boys at Christmas?

France: Ah, oui – Père Noel … Father Christmas.

Minister:	And do the boys and girls in France hang up their stockings at Christmas?
France:	No, they put their shoes beside the fireplace and they put a carrot in them for Père Noel's donkey.
Minister:	Père Noel's donkey?
France:	Oui, Father Christmas does not use reindeer in France. He uses a donkey to deliver his gifts, and he puts the gifts in the shoes of the girls and boys.
Minister:	Well, now, Aubagne, it is time for your carol. What is its name?
France:	'Il est né le divine enfant', or, as you would say in English, 'Born on Earth is the Child Divine'

[*Children sing a verse in English after a solo verse sung in French.*]

◆ HYMN – 'Il est né Le Divine Enfant' –
no. 24, *Folk Carols for Young Children* [Wardlock Educational Publishers]

Minister:	Bien. Beautiful. But now we are off to the mountains of Austria, to the famous ski resort of Innsbruck, where the Winter Olympics have been held. Guten Morgen, again, Innsbruck.
Austria:	Guten Morgen, Schottland. What is the weather like with you?
Minister:	[*Replies truthfully!*]
Austria:	Here it is sharp and crisp, the air clear with snow covering the mountains. A good day for the krippe.

Minister:	The krippe?

Austria:	Yes, our children make little nativity crib-scenes. We call them *krippe*. One child goes in front with a pole and a star fixed to it. The rest of the children follow, one carrying the krippe. They go from house to house, singing 'Star' songs. When they find a house without a krippe, they give their krippe to them and in return they are given gifts.

Minister:	What a lovely idea. And I suppose you will have Christmas trees as we do?

Austria:	Yes, this is the land of the Christmas tree and we decorate them with lights, white lights, not coloured lights like yours. And on the door of each house we put a wreath of laurel or holly with red berries on it to remind us of the life that came into the world in Jesus.

Minister:	Well, now, Austria, what carol do you have for our service today?

Austria:	Ah, well, what other carol could we sing, but that carol that has gone all the way around the world, 'Stille Nacht'?

◆ HYMN – 'Stille Nacht' ('Still the Night')
no. 176 [*CH3*]

Minister:	Now, for a little while, we leave our friends on the continent of Europe, though we'll return to them, and go instead to Nicaragua in South America. What's the weather like in Nicaragua – cold and frosty?

Nicaragua: No, no, Scotland. It is summer here. This is the time when our flowers are very beautiful and so our churches are decorated with flowers.

Minister: How lovely. But tell me, Nicaragua, what is pasada? Every time I hear of Christmas in South America, I hear of pasada. What is it?

Nicaragua: It is a custom in our villages. One house is chosen as the pasada, or lodging, just like the inn in which Jesus was born. Everyone goes around the village looking for it and at each home they sing Christmas carols. When they come to the house with the crib, they place a doll in it as the Christ-child and worship and celebrate his birth, finishing with a feast and a party.

Minister: That sounds marvellous fun. So is it one of these carols that you might sing at pasada that you are going to sing for us today?

Nicaragua: Yes, our carol is one we might sing to the sleeping child in the crib.

◆ HYMN – 'Sleep quietly, my Jesus' –
no. 25, *Carol, Gaily Carol* [A & C Black]

Minister: Now it's back from far away South America to Europe again, to the Czech Republic. Versek vannoch, Prague.

Prague: Versek vannoch, Boglemart Sound. We have been listening with interest to the carols and customs of all these other countries. We too have our customs. For instance, we have a much longer Christmas than you. Christmas starts for our children on the 5th of December, the Eve of St Nicholas. That evening the children receive presents

117

of apples and nuts and candles. The boys go round the village with little carved wooden flexible playthings with the head of a snake. As they go to each house, they wave the snakes in the air. Everyone gives them a present.

Minister: So they make the snakes themselves?

Prague: Yes.

Minister: Well, they deserve their gifts. Now, what is your carol?

Prague: We call it, 'The Carol of the Drum'. You, I think, call it, 'The Little Drummer Boy'.

◆ HYMN – 'The Little Drummer Boy' –
no. 11, *Carol, Gaily Carol* [A & C Black]

Minister: Please thank your drummer, Prague. Now, I wonder what Barbados has in store for us?

Barbados: Well, I'm afraid we don't have a drum. But here in the West Indies we celebrate Christmas too and we love rhythm. I think you will like our carol, 'Mary had a Baby'.

◆ HYMN – 'Mary had a Baby' –
no. 2, *Carol, Gaily Carol* [A & C Black]

Barbados: What did you think of that Scotland? Was everyone swaying to the rhythm?

Minister: Yes, indeed we were.

Barbados: But now, Scotland, it is your turn. Can you tell us something of what YOU do at Christmas?

Minister: Certainly, Barbados. I have one of the children here beside me now, so I'm going to ask her what she's going to be doing at Christmas.

[*A live interview.*]

Barbados: Thank you [........ *name of interviewee*]. What is your carol, Scotland?

Minister: The Scottish Carol, 'Child in the Manger'.

◆ HYMN – 'Child in the Manger' –
no. 180 [*CH3*]

Minister: That carol brings to an end our international broadcast for the Sunday before Christmas. It has been wonderful to join with our friends all round the world to learn what they do at Christmas and to celebrate Jesus' birth with their carols. We have learned that the world is one in celebration. Let us never forget that. Let us join together now, wherever we are, in singing a carol that takes all of us back to childhood, 'Away in a Manger'. Goodbye world. And Merry Christmas!

[*Each place replies with their original Christmas greeting.*]

◆ HYMN – 'Away in a Manger' –
no. 195 [*CH3*]

Producer: [*As red light goes off on table, gives thumbs up to everybody*] Well done, everybody!

Minister: [*A thanks to everybody and the Benediction.*]

A Service
for the New Year

[A slightly shorter service because it fell on New Year's Day itself.]

◆ HYMN –
'Great is Thy Faithfulness' –
no. 3, Songs of God's People [Oxford University Press]

◆ READING – Revelation 21: 1-7

◆ PRAYER –

[There is a loud knocking on one of the doors of the Church. The minister gradually draws attention to it.]

Minister: Can you hear something? Is that someone knocking at the door? Mr .... , could you please go and see if there is someone at the door?

[The person appointed goes to the door but does not return with the person knocking, until the minister has read the following poem.]

Minister:

> Who is that knocking at the door?
> Could it be someone that we know?
> Or could it be our cousin Fred?
> Or even long-lost brother Ned?

Maybe its Auntie Jane from Troon,
Or Uncle Ben back from the moon?
Perhaps it is the parcel post,
The butcher delivering meat to roast?
It could be none of them at all,
Only a handsome stranger tall.
Or perhaps I was quite mistaken
It is the wind some mischief making.
And yet, I'm sure, as sure can be
It's someone come to visit ME!

Mr .... :   You're right, Mr Roy. There *was* someone knocking at the door. [*Turns to someone behind the door*] Come on in. [*The visitor enters.*]

Minister: Oh, please, do come in and take a seat. [*The visitor makes his way to a seat near the front where he can be seen by the congregation.*] I'm glad we heard you knocking. Were you knocking long?

Visitor: No.

Minister: That's good. It would be terrible if you had knocked and we had not heard. Jesus once said, '*Listen, I stand at the door and knock. If anyone hears my voice and opens the door, I will come into his house and eat with him, and he will eat with me*' [Revelation 3: 20, GNB]. Wouldn't it be terrible if Jesus were to be knocking at the door of our home, or our Church, or our heart, and we did not hear, or, worse still, heard but did not let Him in? Jesus is always at the door of our hearts, wanting to come in with His love and His truth. But we have to let Him in!

'Come into my heart, Lord Jesus
There is room in my heart for you.'

121

◆ HYMN –
'Lord Jesus Christ, You have come to Us' –
no. 2, *Songs of God's People* [Oxford University Press]

Visitor: But Mr Roy, I was knocking at the door for a reason. Don't you remember what day this is? It's NEW YEAR'S DAY!

Minister: Yes, I know, but what difference does that make?

Visitor: Well, I've come to first foot you.

Minister: Oh, you'll have to excuse me. I just thought you were late for Church!

Visitor: No, no. I've brought you a gift.

[*Comes up to the pulpit with a polythene bag from which he produces a lump of coal. Goes back to his seat.*]

Minister: Oh, wasn't that nice? This is a traditional gift for New Year. The first foot, dark-haired, brings a piece of coal. We still do the same, only it is probably a box of chocolates, or some shortbread, a bunch of flowers or a plant. But we still first foot to show friendship.

When Jesus came into the world at Christmas, he also brought a gift as proof of his friendship for us – God's love. And later on in his life Jesus told people why he had come into the world: *'I am come that you might have life'* [John 10: 10, GNB]. To live, we need more than food to eat, clothes to wear, or coal or gas to heat our house. We need God's love – to show us HOW to live.

◆ HYMN –
'Love came down at Christmas' –
no. 194, *CH3* [Oxford University Press]

Minister: But here, I have forgotten my manners. This poor chap
came to first foot me, and I've been rambling on and
forgetting to be a good host. What do we do when someone comes to first foot us? Yes, we give them something
to eat and drink. Perhaps, girls and boys, you would
help me to do the honours?

[*He chooses some of the children to go and fetch glasses, a bottle of ginger
wine, and a plate with some bun and some shortbread. The children, the
minister, and the visitor, all toast each other and eat.*]

Minister: [*Back in pulpit*] The Apostle said, '*Keep on loving one
another as Christian brethren. Remember to welcome strangers
to your homes. There were some who did that and welcomed
angels without knowing it*' [Hebrews 13: 2, GNB]. Hospi-
tality is a very important thing for Christians to give – at
New Year we all get an opportunity to practise it. And
in Church especially we have to remember, not only
today, but every Sunday, to be welcoming to everyone
who comes here, especially the stranger and the visitor,
and offer them the same love that God in Jesus has
offered us by the coming of his son.

◆ OFFERING –

◆ OFFERTORY PRAYER AND INTERCESSIONS –

Minister: Did you notice that when we wished each other a Happy
New Year we shook hands? Shaking hands is a very
important gesture. It says to people, without our even
speaking, 'I want to get to know you. I want to find out

who you are. I want to offer you my friendship and open up myself to you'. Jesus by his coming offers us the same – God's outstretched hand of love and friendship.

It's the same hand he stretches out to us today at the start of a New Year as he gave to us in the Year that has gone. A good New Year to you and may God be with you all the way.

[*The congregation are invited to greet each other by hand.*]

◆ HYMN –
'Now thank We all Our God' –
no. 368, *CH3* [Oxford University Press]

◆ BENEDICTION –

Palm Sunday

◆ HYMN –
'Praise to the Holiest in the Height' –
no. 238, *CH3* [Oxford University Press]

◆ READING – Mark 1: 16-20

◆ PRAYER –

◆ HYMN –
'Hosanna, Loud Hosanna' –
no. 235, *CH3* [Oxford University Press]

FIRST SECTION – THE FISH

Minister: Well, it will not be long until everyone has their Easter
holidays. I would not mind a holiday myself. I really
feel I need one.

[*As he speaks, he has begun to fish with a stick that has a string attached
to it with a bent pin at the end of it. In my case I was fishing over the side
of the choir area and down a grating on the floor!*]

A.N. Other: Mr Roy, what are you doing?

Minister: Surely that's obvious – I'm fishing.

125

A.N. Other: But you cannot fish here.

Minister: Of course I can. When its high tide at the shore, the water comes up here right under the Church [or *there's a pool underneath the Church itself.*]

A.N. Other: I don't believe you *can* fish here anyway.

Minister: Oh, yes, I can. In fact I will show you how I used to fish when I was a wee boy. Perhaps you would like to see.

[*Encourages A.N. Other to come and see him guddling for fish. Rolls up his sleeve and commences – and, as A.N. Other is watching closely, suddenly rises with a brown paper fish in his hands that he has a struggle to keep hold of and splashes some water in the face of A.N. Other at the same time.*]

A.N. Other: [*Spluttering.*] What kind of fish is that?

Minister: Can't you see? It's a BROWN trout, a brown paper trout! But tell them about THE FISH.

A.N. Other: [*He puts up the Greek word for fish – ICTHUS – and then, begins to explain the code.*]

I	[ESOUS]	JESUS
C	[HRISTOS]	CHRIST
TH	[EOU]	GOD'S
U	[IOS]	SON
S	[OTER]	SAVIOUR

Minister: So the fish became a secret sign in the Early Church. Christians were being persecuted and put to death. People used the sign of the fish to tell each other in a kind of code that they were followers of Jesus.

A.N. Other: But, of course, today we don't want to keep it a secret. We want to tell people that we have heard the Good News of Jesus Christ and especially so in Holy Week – the Week in which Jesus died to save us all.

◆ HYMN –
'When Jesus saw the Fishermen' –
no. 230, *CH3* [Oxford University Press]

SECOND SECTION

Minister: Cock-a-doodle-doo! [*repeats the sign*]

A.N. Other: What a racket! Why are you making that noise?

Minister: Because I think we should tell the girls and boys about this fine fellow [*putting up the picture of a cock*]. Do you know who he is? Yes, the cock. Do you know the nursery rhyme about the cock?

[*Recites: 'Cock-a-doodle-doo, My dame has lost her shoe'.*]

A.N. Other: Every morning the cock makes its noise and wakens people up. So, the cock became a sign of watchfulness. Jesus told Christians that they were to be watchful, always looking for his coming, looking for God, seeing when God has something for them to do.

Minister: There's a story about a cock in the last week of Jesus' life. Let me read the story to you

◆ READING – Mark 14: 66-72

A.N. Other: Peter betrayed Jesus, and when he did the cock crowed, just as Jesus said it would, three times. How ashamed Peter must have felt to do this to his friend. But then, that is what Holy Week teaches us – that it is easy for any one of us to let Jesus down. But Jesus died in Holy Week to forgive us and to give us a fresh start to follow him more closely.

Minister: Do you know why on the spires of many churches cocks are used as weather-vanes? Well, they were put there as a warning to those who pass by, not to do as Peter did and betray Jesus. Cock-a-doodle-doo, says the cock. 'Watch and don't sin'!

◆ HYMN –
'Do no Sinful Action' –
no. 663, *CH2* [Oxford University Press]

◆ OFFERING –

THIRD SECTION

[*A.N. Other is in the pulpit, letting down a cardboard anchor on a rope.*]

Minister: What *are* you doing?

A.N. Other: I'm letting down this ANCHOR. Did you know that the anchor was one of the earliest symbols used in the Christian Church? It was a sign put on Christian graves in the catacombs, the caves under Rome where the early Christians used to hide from their persecutors. I wonder if the girls and boys can see why? Well, if you look closely, you will see that an anchor looks very much like a cross.

| Minister: | But Paul also spoke about Faith as an Anchor. The Boys' Brigade chose it as their badge and they sing about it in their famous hymn. |

◆ READING – Hebrews 6: 18-19

◆ HYMN –
'Will Your Anchor hold?' –
no. 412, *CH3* [Oxford University Press]

FOURTH SECTION

| A.N. Other: | The most famous Christian sign of all is the cross. Do you know that the cross is perhaps the most popular piece of jewellery worn by ladies today? You can buy it in gold, or silver, or even encrusted with jewels. |

| Minister: | But the first cross was not like that at all. [*Displays a simple wooden cross.*] It was a cross made of wood, like this one, but large enough for Jesus' body to be nailed to it by cruel men. There on Calvary Jesus died upon the cross to show the world how much God loves us. Above the cross they wrote in three languages: 'Jesus of Nazareth, the King of the Jews'. But, of course, that was not true. Jesus was not the King of the Jews, But he *is* the KING of KINGS. |

| A.N. Other: | The one we follow as the fishermen did. |

| Minister: | The one who asks us to be watchful, not to betray him, but to follow him closely. |

| A.N. Other: | The one who holds us fast in his care like the anchor holds the ship – safely. |

129

Minister: The one who died on the cross to show us that his love would go to any length to save us. Write that upon your hearts this Holy Week and remember *how* he loves you.

◆ PRAYER –

◆ HYMN –
'In the Cross of Christ I glory' –
no. 259, *CH3* [Oxford University Press]

◆ BENEDICTION –

A
Project Service

[The project was a study of Africa and the life of David Livingstone. It preceded a visit to the birthplace at Blantyre and was intended as a preparation for the visit and for the project which had been devised by the Sunday School. The service is just a simple story approach. There is still a place for stories in worship and the presentation of facts.]

◆ HYMN –

◆ PRAYER –

◆ READING – *[by one of the children]*
  Matthew 28: 16-20

FIRST SECTION – THE DARK CONTINENT

Minister: Girls and boys, I've put a map on this blackboard. It's a strange map. Maps usually show you where rivers run, and roads go, where mountains and valleys are. But this is a blank map. Can you tell me which continent it is a map of? Yes, Africa.

But I wonder why it is not only a blank map, but a Black Map *[the whole map was cut out of black paper]*? The colour of the people? Yes. But also because Africa was the dark continent, the unknown continent. Long ago, people did not know where the rivers ran on this continent, how high the mountains were, where even the paths led. They called it 'The Dark Continent' because it was unknown. But even what *was* known made it seem savage, strange, hostile.

Africa is a very large continent. Much bigger than most people imagine. AFRICA equals Europe plus China plus India plus the whole of the United States of America in size!

One wee Scots boy grew up to love this great continent and to do a great deal to make it known to other people. In a minute or two I am going to tell you about him, but first we are going to sing a hymn. But for this you will have to learn some African. Let's start with 'KUM BA YAH'. Can you say that? Right, now you can *sing* it.

◆ HYMN –
'Kum Bah Yah'

SECOND SECTION – A LITTLE SCOTS BOY

Minister: Does anyone here have their birthday on the 19th of March? If you do, you share your birthday with some- one very famous. On the 19th of March 1813 a little boy called David was born in Blantyre in Scotland, in his grandpa's house. Soon you are going to visit that house where David Livingstone was born and we will see how it would look then. There were twenty-four houses in the building, single kitchens, where all the family lived and slept and ate.

132

Beside the houses stood a mill where the people who lived in the houses worked. Is there any boy here who is ten years old? Would you come out? Let's see how strong you are [*feeling his upper arm muscles*]. I wanted to see if you were strong enough to go to work. David Livingstone was only ten when he went to work in the mill. Before that, he went to school just as you do. After work he went to night school. He finished work at 8 p.m. and then spent two hours at night school. Sometimes when he came home, he went on studying until midnight.

His job was to tie broken threads in the spinning mill. Sometimes he would read in between times, setting up his book like this on the machine. The girls used to throw bobbins at it to see if they could knock it down. Anyone like to try?

When he did have free time, Livingstone loved to walk in the country and collect plants and stones. He became a great observer of things.

David Livingstone worked for thirteen years in the thread mill, and then he went to the Anderson College to learn to be a doctor, finishing his training in London. He was twenty-seven when he became a doctor. The wee Scots boy was now grown up. Just think – some day you will be *twenty-seven!*

◆ HYMN –
'One More Step along the World I go' –
no. 90, *Songs of God's People* [Oxford University Press]

THIRD SECTION – OPENING UP AFRICA

Minister: David Livingstone might never have been in Africa. He really wanted to go to China, but, when that was impossible, he decided to go to Africa. There he met a missionary called Dr James Moffatt, his future father-in-law, and he asked him, 'Will I do for Africa?'

'Yes,' replied Dr Moffatt, 'if you are prepared to leave occupied ground and press on to the north.'

Very soon that was what Livingstone was doing, going not just north but east and west as well. He travelled with African people. They took him on little paths, some just 37 centimetres or 15 inches wide. [*Measure it with the children.*]

If a tree fell, or an ant-hill was on the path, they just had to walk round it. As he went, Livingstone kept a journal. In it he drew little maps of the countryside and described what he saw. He began to look for the lakes and the rivers and the mountains. Soon Livingstone was making it possible for people to make maps of Africa, to make maps like this instead of the blank map that we started with.

[*Put up a map of Africa with detail, or, in white pen fill in the black map with some details,* eg *rivers.*]

Livingstone began to make Africa *known* to the world, and not just Africa but the people of Africa. Livingstone loved the black people who journeyed with them. He discovered something we should know also – that God loves all the people of the world, whatever their colour.

◆ HYMN – 'The Ink is Black' –
no. 39, *Someone's Singing, Lord*

FOURTH SECTION – THE PROBLEMS OF AFRICA

Minister: As Livingstone travelled around Africa, he came across something very terrible happening to his black brothers and sisters. He found great numbers of them moving along these same paths as himself, But they were chained and manacled to each other, or they had a wooden shackle around their necks. They were being cruelly whipped by their captors, evil Arab slavetraders who were selling them into captivity in Zanzibar. From there, they were shipped by white people, who looked like Livingstone himself, into slavery. Livingstone called this cruel trade the 'Open Sore of Africa'. In the years that followed, he did everything he could to make sure that the whole world knew about this great problem of Africa so that something could be done to stop it. Eventually it was stopped.

Africa still has great problems, the 'open sores' of Africa today – hunger, poverty, slaughter and persecution, injustice and cruelty. David Livingstone would still want us to do something about it, and so does God. We can do something. We can pray for Africa. We can give to Africa through Christian Aid, Oxfam and the Tear Fund. We must make sure that the Dark Continent – and our own continent too – has LIGHT ... THE LIGHT OF GOD'S LOVE.

◆ OFFERING AND PRAYER –

◆ CLOSING HYMN AND BENEDICTION –

135

Acknowledgements

Unless otherwise stated, biblical quotations used within this book are taken from the REVISED STANDARD VERSION (RSV), copyright 1946, 1952, © 1971, by the Division of Christian Education of the National Council of Churches of Christ in the USA, and are used by permission.

For the historical details upon which the Talks entitled 'The Floating Church' and 'The Betsy' were based, the author acknowledges Thomas Brown DD: *Annals of the Disruption, 1843* (Edinburgh: McNiven and Wallace, 1893).

While all reasonable efforts have been made to trace and to acknowledge sources, the publisher apologises if any have been missed inadvertently. This will be amended at the next printing.

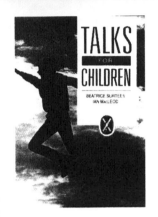
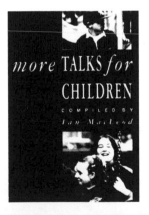